ROBERT LOUIS STEVENSON
&
FRANCE

Louis Stott

CREAG DARACH PUBLICATIONS

For Leila

ISBN 1 874585 03 2

Published by
Creag Darach Publications
Milton of Aberfoyle
FK8 3TD
(0877) 382476

Printed by
Cordfall
041 332 4640

Contents

RLS: portrait by Krøyer

Introduction

The aim of this book is to treat RLS's associations with France as a whole. It is hoped that it will appeal both to the general reader, to Stevenson enthusiasts, and to readers perhaps more familiar with France than with Stevenson who will enjoy his love affair with that country.

Robert Louis Stevenson (1850-94) wrote four books, any one of which would have immortalised him: *Travels with a Donkey in the Cévennes*, largely written in France, *Treasure Island, Dr Jekyll and Mr Hyde*, and *Kidnapped*. What most critics suspect might have been his best book, *Weir of Hermiston*, was unfinished when he died. However, he wrote many other short stories, novels, essays and poems, some of which literary critics perceive as being, in their way, of better quality, or more intriguing than the books which made him famous. Of his poetry *A Child's Garden of Verses*, about half of which were composed in France, is not far short of the four books already mentioned in having secured him a lasting reputation.

He is one of the three or four best known Scottish authors, and a British literary giant. He is interesting as a person as well as a writer, in part at least, because of his cosmopolitan qualities. He spent much time in France and his American step-son, Lloyd Osbourne, considered him 'more than half French'. He went to the United States where he is thought of as a significant American author, and it might be said that one fact which is universally known about him is that, like Gauguin, he went to the South Seas. A similar aura to that associated with the painter surrounds him on that account. He was multi-national.

RLS was dogged by ill-health. He was a delicate child whose schooling was interrupted. Many of his journeys were undertaken as an invalid. He suffered from pulmonary tuberculosis, probably inherited from his mother, and spent much of his life trying to beat it. He did not die from the disease, but from a cerebral haemorrhage, and, although signs of TB appeared early on, Stevenson lived until he was forty-four. He can thus be said to have had some resistance to it, and to have fought it spiritedly. Medical men consider that, had his case been managed by modern methods, TB might never have overtaken him, or it would probably have been arrested.

The debilitating disease from which he suffered affected him in many ways: he was sometimes depressed, although there were periods of elation; he was prevented from working and, worse, his work was often interrupted at a critical stage by ill-health. There is no substance in the suggestion that his genius was in some way connected with TB, as has been asserted in more than one book. However, his illnesses – which, in addition to TB, included ophthalmia, nervous exhaustion and sciatica – governed his life.

RLS made light of his health. An interesting illustration of this in a French context is provided by Eugénie Hamerton [Gindriez], whom RLS visited in Autun:

> Knowing that he had lately been dangerously ill, I ventured to express my fear that the smoking of endless cigarettes might prove injurious. 'Oh, I don't know,' he said; 'and yet I daresay it is; but you see, Mrs Hamerton, as there are only a very limited number of things enjoyable to an individual in this world, these must be enjoyed to the utmost; and if I knew smoking would kill me, still I would not give it up, for I shall surely die of something, very likely not so pleasant.'
> [Memoir of Philip Gilbert Hamerton]

It was the state of his health which first took Stevenson to France as a young man, but his many visits to France for some time thereafter arose from inclination. He had begun to train as an engineer, but he gave that up, and, when he first went to France, he was studying, rather desultorily, to be an advocate. However, he really wanted to be a writer, and this exacerbated the difficult relationship which he had with his father as a young adult. These difficulties arose, partly from outlook and temperament,

Autun: the hamlet where P. G. Hamerton lived

but partly from serious differences of opinion, for example, about religion. He perceived a need to distance himself from home, and he saw the 'Capital of Art' as a highly attractive place to learn to write.

The treatment of Stevenson's visits to France by his biographers is necessarily episodic. Furthermore the popularity, at different times, of *An Inland Voyage* and *Travels with a Donkey* has perhaps given readers a rather strange impression of Stevenson's connections with France. His long grounding in Menton, where he was taken as a boy on account of his mother's health, may be overlooked, and accounts of the dramatic developments in his personal life in Paris and at Grès tend to neglect the cultural context in which they took place.

Stevenson was very fond indeed of France. In *On the Trail of Stevenson* Clayton Hamilton put it thus, 'Stevenson lived more freely, more fully, and more happily in France than in any other country', and he went on, 'Louis was Gallic in his nimbleness of gesture, his mobility of face, his enthusiastic eloquence of conversation, his gaiety of spirit, his lust for freedom and adventure.'

Charles Sarolea, a Professor of French at Edinburgh University, put in a cautionary note at about the same time as Hamilton:

'The attraction which drew Stevenson to France might easily
be misunderstood.'

He went on to point out that it was not elective affinities which attracted
him to France, but the attraction of opposites. In French literature, in French
art and in French culture generally, he saw qualities and characteristics
which he did not possess which he admired.

Be that as it may, Lloyd Osbourne, an acute observer of his step-
father, characterised him as follows, in an introduction to *New Arabian
Nights*:

> France had a profound influence over Stevenson; mentally
> he was half a Frenchman; in taste, habits, and prepossessions
> he was almost wholly French. Not only did he speak French
> admirably and read it like his mother-tongue, but he loved
> both country and people, and was more really at home in
> France than anywhere else.

Thus Osbourne picks up the key to any consideration of Stevenson
and France. He was not simply one of the long succession of British
authors infatuated with France, he was shaped by France. For this reason
he is loved and respected in France. There are those who hold that
Stevenson never grew up, and it can safely be said that he took a long
time to mature. At twenty-three he embarked on a period of five years
when he went to France whenever he could. He was a Bohemian when
to be a Bohemian – 'a little Murger-mad' – in Paris defined the term,
and he met his future wife there. If he did grow up, Stevenson grew
up in France.

He read and spoke French fluently. He could correspond in French
with his French friends. Fanny Stevenson put it thus:

> ...in Mentone, the child acquired an accent and vocabulary
> that remained with him all the rest of his life. He knew little
> of French grammar (or, indeed, of any grammar) but spoke
> the vernacular with a freedom and accuracy which caused
> him to be accepted everywhere by the French as one of
> themselves, though perhaps from another province. [Prefatory
> Note to *An Inland Voyage*]

There is no better illustration of Stevenson's familiarity with France
and French than a story re-told by Andrew Lang: 'In Paris, at a café,

Grèz: the view from the Hôtel Chevillon of the old tower and the church; the walled garden of Delius's house is between the two

I remember that Mr Stevenson heard a Frenchman say that the English were cowards. He got up, and slapped the man's face.

"Monsieur, vous m'avez frappé!" said the Gaul.

"A ce qu'il paraît [So it seems]," said the Scot, and there it ended.

If one supposes this story to be exact, it illustrates both a nimbleness of intellect in a foreign tongue, and a carelessness about the consequences of one's actions which epitomise Stevenson.

After a period of five years from 1874 to 1879 when he was much in France he went to America, and got married. When he returned to Europe his health deteriorated. To his everlasting regret the climate of his beloved Scotland exacerbated his symptoms, and he spent much of his adult life in various resorts abroad. He became, as a consequence, something of a connoisseur of health resorts. In his native land he had gone as a youth to Bridge of Allan and to Dunblane, and he later tried Strathpeffer, the northerly Scottish spa. On the Continent he had become familiar with the resorts of the Mediterranean coast, particularly the 'English' resorts of Menton, where he spent three winters, and Nice.

He also stayed for long periods in the early eighteen-eighties in Davos in Switzerland, and went twice to Royat. However, he and his wife set up their first real home in 1883/4 in Hyères. There was a further visit to Paris in 1886, and an oft expressed intention of returning to France. There was, too, in the South Seas, a link with France in visits to French possessions overseas, but, to his great regret, Stevenson was never in France again.

Stevenson and French Literature

> I have found here a new friend to whom I grow daily more
> devoted, George Sand. I go on from one novel to another,
> and think the last I have read the most sympathetic and friendly
> in tone, until I have read another. It is a life in dreamland.
> [*Letters*]

Stevenson, the cosmopolitan, first read Dostoevsky in French. His enthusiasm
for English literature rapidly extended to the literature of other countries,
above all of France. He used books in a variety of ways. As an invalid
he was an avid reader, except when ophthalmia or worse prevented him.
He used them as models when he was learning to write. He used them
to educate himself about history, and as the sources of ideas. His most
important literary friendships, with Edmund Gosse, with Henry James and
with Andrew Lang, were built, in part at least, on the exchange of books,
and opinions about books. He loved the libraries of Paris, although the
officials on occasion frustrated him. He liked pottering in bookshops, or
among bookstalls. There can be little doubt that the respect which he is
accorded in France is at least partly due to his delight in French writing.
He could correspond in French, and his books were translated into French
early on.

Charles Sarolea, Professor of French at the University of Edinburgh in
the nineteen-twenties commented in *Robert Louis Stevenson and France*:
"It is difficult to over-estimate Stevenson's sympathy with the French spirit,
and the wide range of his French reading." He goes on, as a Professor
of French would, to lament RLS's lack of discipline in the matter, pointing

out the gaps in what he did read – he appears, Sarolea points out, not to have read 'the classics of the golden age of French literature, the seventeenth century', and that 'the French literature of the eighteenth century was to him "terra incognita"'.

Stevenson was perfectly well aware of this, calling himself, at one point, a 'literary vagrant', and RLS was an original, not afraid to imitate French stylists in trying to improve his own techniques, and not afraid, even as a comparatively young man, to try to write authoritatively about French authors, recommending authors he enjoyed for general consumption. He was perfectly modest about this, acknowledging that his opinions might not be shared by everyone, but he was also sufficiently confident to consider that, for example, in some instances, he understood what French poets meant, better than their august translators did.

He mastered the language when he was young, and his long sojourns in France meant that he began to devour many works of particular authors. He always asserted that he derived a great deal from Montaigne, the great essayist, but, almost as if he was rationing himself, he also pointed out that he had never read all of him:

> At an early date Stevenson's admiration of Montaigne leads him on to the study of Sainte Beuve. For Sainte Beuve's literary criticism is like Montaigne's philosophy, it is mainly a criticism of life. Already in 1872, Stevenson buys Sainte Beuve's two volumes on Chateaubriand and declares himself highly delighted with them, although the subject of the book, namely Chateaubriand, is more antipathetic to him than any one else in the world. [Sarolea]

Sarolea provides a long analysis of Stevenson and Montaigne in the latter part of his book.

In the year when he first went to Barbizon, 1875, Stevenson, who had already published a study, which he had written in Menton, of Victor Hugo's *Romances*, wrote an article for the *Encyclopaedia Britannica* about Pierre-Jean Béranger (1780-1857), a French poet, the author of popular light verse, which, although it is sometimes dismissed as slight, displayed both his interest in, and the depth of his knowledge of, French literature.

That year, too, RLS was busy studying two other French poets, Charles d'Orléans (1391-1465), and François Villon (b.1431). Enthusiasm for these two was fashionable then – Andrew Lang had translated them into English, for example, and George Moore makes reference to Villon. During his tramp through the Gâtinais RLS imagined that he was Villon, a fugitive from Paris and strode through the Gâtinais composing 'roundels' (rondeaux), a verse-form popular with several other C19 British and French poets, in the style of these early poets. Two of his efforts survive in a letter.

In the following year *Cornhill* published his more substantial essay about Charles d'Orléans, and the year after that another on François Villon. These works were undoubtedly the product, in part, of the time he spent in Fontainebleau, at Barbizon and Grèz, although, *Charles of Orleans*, for example, occupied him for more than twelve months. A letter, which he wrote to Colvin from Edinburgh in the autumn of 1875, indicates the elaborate web of research which the young Stevenson undertook in Scotland, in France, and elsewhere, in producing these apparently slight pieces:

> Meantime when I have done Burns, I shall finish Charles of Orleans (who is in a good way, about the fifth of the month, I should think, and promises to be a fine healthy child, better than any of his elder brothers for a while); and then, perhaps, Villon, for Villon is a very essential part of my Ramsay-Ferguson-Burns; I mean is a note in it, and will recur again and again for comparison and illustration; then perhaps I may try Fontainebleau [*Forest Notes*] by the way.

Villon was the subject, too, of *A Lodging for the Night* his first successful short story, which came out the same autumn [1877]. He retained his enthusiasm for Villon until the end of his life, writing to Marcel Schwob (1867-1905) in 1891, he said:

> Whatever you do, do not neglect to send me what you publish on Villon: I look forward to that with lively interest.

Both Béranger and Villon probably appealed to him because they were rebels, poets involved, in one way and another, in politics. He came to dislike Villon, but his essay brought Villon to the attention of others in a significant way. The best book about Villon, a delicious book in itself, quirky in its approach, but everything a book ought to be, readable, of course, but also beautifully designed and printed, is D.B. Wyndham Lewis's *François Villon*. At the very beginning of it the author pays, in these circumstances, an immense tribute to Stevenson.

One can fairly safely conclude that RLS's essays about Victor Hugo, about Béranger, about Villon and about Charles d'Orléans, and, for that matter, his later *Gossip on a Novel of Dumas* [1887] arose from his own enthusiasms, and from his perception, as a writer, that it was almost his duty, if he could, to explain to others just what their importance was. As an indication of his approach we can refer to *Charles of Orleans*. Scotland is never far from his thoughts. Describing the poet-prince's stately progress in a barge along the Loire he is reminded of the Crinan Canal. He also reminds us that 'in the year 1415 Henry V had two distinguished prisoners, French Charles of Orleans and Scottish James I, who whiled away their captivity with rhyming.' RLS speculates about the frame of mind of prisoner-poets: 'With what regret Scottish James I bethought him (in the next room perhaps to Charles) of the time when he rose 'early as the day'. What would he not have given to wet his boots once more with morning dew, and follow his vagrant fancy among the meadows? The only alleviation to the misery of constraint lies in the disposition of the prisoner.'

We can note that he did not try to explain Montaigne, and this was surely wise, for every teacher, particularly if she or he is a writer, should keep, for her or himself, a secret territory, to sustain them. Explanations for such enthusiasms must be left to the likes of Sarolea.

His voyages into French literature had other purposes. He read Chateaubriand, a Catholic, and others including, Napoléon Peyrat (1809-81), because he wanted to understand the fate of French Protestants. He read Michelet, carrying a copy with him on the walking tour already referred to, because he wanted to understand France. He eventually read critics and philosophers like Taine and Renan to understand the world. He reads Molière for pleasure, and he reads his contemporaries, like Anatole France, to find out what they are up to. Sarolea is dismissive of some of his passions for C19 French authors, for Jules Amadée Barbey d'Aurevilly (1808-1889) the poet, and novelist, for Alfred de Musset (1810-57) as a writer of comedies, and for Alphonse Daudet (1840-97) the contemporary Provençal essayist and dramatist, whom RLS characterised as 'the best of the present French novelists'. One can see in the latter something of Stevenson, and understand why he appealed to him. Sarolea is more approving of Stevenson's admiration, stated in 1874, for Flaubert's style, and understanding of his passion for George Sand rather than George Eliot. He is disconcerted by RLS's enthusiasm for Dumas (père). These enthusiasms were accompanied by dislikes. RLS often criticised Balzac's writing, and he did not admire Emile Zola, although he acknowledged his power.

When Stevenson was in Paris, Low reports that there were 'interminable discussions concerning Balzac, Théodore de Banville, or Villon on life or conduct'. Théodore Faullin de Banville (1823-91), the poet, published *Trente-six ballades joyeuses à la manière de François Villon* [1873] and *Rondels à la manière de Charles d'Orléans* [1875], so we can appreciate why RLS was interested in him. Stevenson's poem which begins 'Nous n'irons plus au bois...' is a paraphrase of Banville. As with Scott everyone read Balzac, but RLS permitted his principal character in *The Wrecker* to say to himself that 'We were all a little Murger-mad in those days'. Henry Murger (1822-

61) novelist and poet, the author of *La Vie de Bohème*, was also translated by Lang, and was extremely fashionable at that time.

Lang – who knew Stevenson, whereas Sarolea did not – tells us that 'Mr Stevenson had an infinite pleasure in Boisgobey, Montépin, and, of course, Gaboriau.' This sheds a different light on him, because these forgotten authors were the popular novelists of the day. Xavier de Montépin (1823-1902) wrote serials for the popular papers, Emile Gaboriau (1832-73) was the father of the 'roman policier', the Edgar Alan Poe of France, and Fortuné Duboisgobey (1821-1891) was a prolific writer of sensational novels with titles like *The Severed Hand* whose works occupy many columns of the British Library catalogue. Lang relates that he and Stevenson once plotted a 'Boisgobesque' story together. There was to be a prisoner in a Muscovite dungeon from whom information was to be extracted with corkscrews!

Stevenson's involvement with French literature never waned. He still has his enthusiasms, discovering Paul Bourget (1852-1935), the novelist, travel writer and critic, whom he dubbed 'exquisite', in the South Seas in 1891. He dedicated *Across the Plains* to him. From Sydney he corresponded with Marcel Schwob, later to become a highly respected literary critic, encouraging him, and looking forward to being able to meet him.

Stevenson had a practical admiration for French books, too, at one point insisting to Colvin that his complete works should always be listed opposite the title page after the French fashion.

Writing from Hyères to his cousin Bob about Balzac, he is reminded of Sam Bough, the landscape painter who, unlike Balzac according to RLS, could see just what he wanted to put in a picture. Stevenson was always sure that writers could learn from artists, and when he talked about books it was, we are told by Will Low, often 'in relation to art'. Stevenson's love affair with France may have begun with its books, but it rapidly extended to French Art.

The Black Cat: Steinlen's famous poster for the Paris Night Club

RLS and Scottish and French Art

In the heart of Montmartre during the early eighteen eighties one of the best known café/cabarets stood at No 84 Boulevard Rochechouart. This was the "Chat Noir" founded by Rodolphe Salis, at the door of which was a sign with a cat, representing Art, with its paw on a frightened goose, representing the Bourgeoisie. The motto above the door was "Passant, sois moderne" [Passer-by, be modern]. The cafe-cabaret was frequented by the poets and painters of the day, amongst whom were Toulouse-Lautrec, Louis Anquetin and Théophile Alexandre Steinlen, whose brilliant posters advertised the cabaret. It was one of the most fashionable places in Paris. Salis used to say, "God created the World, Napoleon founded the Legion d'Honneur, and I have established Montmartre." The idea that Salis, who retired with a fortune, should set up a night club originated, according to Birge Harrison, an American artist who wrote his reminiscences, at a meeting in Grèz presided over by Robert Louis Stevenson.

Fernande Sadler, the historian of the artists' colony at Grèz, relates that one evening in 1881 Louis Weldon Hawkins and Frank O'Meara were walking in the Boulevard Clichy, the extension of Boulevard Rochechouart, accompanied by another young painter who frequented Grèz called Rodolphe Salis, when they found a black cat. Rodolphe Salis (1852-1897) had an ambition to open a night-club, and when he swept the cat into his arms his friends proclaimed: "Well, Rodolphe, you have been looking for a name for your cabaret; there it is: 'At the Black Cat'".

Harrison has a slightly different version of this story which connects Rodolphe Salis with Stevenson. Salis first arrived in Grèz in 1875, a refugee from the Commune of 1871 who was arrested and had escaped. Although an amnesty meant that he could return to Paris, he had no means of supporting himself. According to Harrison, Stevenson became Salis's closest friend, so the author called a meeting to consider what could be done about the 'Salis Question'. It was at this meeting that, the sale of drink being a certain way of making money, the idea of starting a cabaret was devised, so it is said, by Stevenson. Harrison further reports that it was because Hawkins had included a black cat in one of his paintings that the name for the place which was eventually adopted was first suggested at the same meeting, but this seems rather too good to be true.

Salis did open the night club, and it enjoyed such a great vogue that it had to be moved to more commodious premises in the Rue Laval, now Rue Victor Massé, where it is commemorated by a plaque:

> Passant Arrète Toi
> Cet Edifice Fut Consacré
> Aux Muses, et À La Joie
> Par
> RODOLPHE SALIS
> Il y logea le fameux
> Cabaret du Chat Noir
> 1885-1896

The "Chat Noir" was most famous for its shadow theatre to which its artist patrons contributed. A room in the Museum of Montmartre is devoted to it. Half a dozen present day establishments perpetuate the name.

Stevenson's connection with the Black Cat may well be apocryphal, but it would have pleased him. RLS was well-educated, cultivated, and interested in the Arts. He moved in circles which meant that he was generally well-informed. As a student aged nineteen, he met Sam Bough (1822-1878), the Cumbrian artist who was at the time one of the leading landscape painters in Scotland, then based in Edinburgh. He and Stevenson remained firm friends, and RLS wrote an affectionate tribute to Bough (which displayed his skills as an art critic) when he died in 1878.

In his early adult life Stevenson's first collaborator, close friend and mentor was William Ernest Henley (1849-1903), poet, dramatist, and editor who, in a multi-faceted professional career, edited the *Magazine of Art*, and was a leading art critic. RLS wrote an article about Fontainebleau, at that time a significant focal point for French Art, which appeared in that journal. Sidney Colvin (1845-1927) became, shortly after he met Stevenson in 1873, Slade Professor of Fine Art in Cambridge and, later, Head of the Print Department at the British Museum. Colvin was older than Stevenson, but very much his loyal friend and adviser. Fanny Sitwell, who later became

Colvin's wife, with whom RLS was then infatuated was both interested in, and informed about art, and Fanny Osbourne, who became his wife, was a convincing amateur who studied painting in a Paris atelier. RLS himself earns an entry in France's principal biographical dictionary of artists, 'Bénézit', in part because of the engravings he produced to illustrate his famous journey across the Cévennes. These were published in Britain in a special edition of *Studio* in 1896/7, but only after his death.

RLS's lifelong interest in art owed much to his cousin Bob, who eventually went to art-school. It meant that RLS had an intellectual sparring partner who became a highly regarded art critic. As young men they were an impressive pair dominating their social group by means of their intellectual talk, their lively wit, and their energetic participation in leisure pursuits. R.A.M. Stevenson (1847-1900) studied painting in Edinburgh, in Antwerp and, giving up both as unsatisfactory, with Carolus-Duran in Paris. Bob was considered a competent painter, but he became more important as a critic. He later wrote influential articles about painting, and a significant book about Velasquez, but perhaps his greatest importance was as an early advocate in Britain of the French Impressionists.

The Gleaners: print, later a painting, of the fields of Fontainebleau, by Millet; the prominence which he gave to the peasants caused controversy

Between 1873 and 1879 RLS was much in France when it was the centre of a revolution in fine art. He was never at the cutting edge of that revolution, but he was one of the liveliest members of a significant community of young artists who followed the Impressionists in Paris and the Forest of Fontainebleau at that time. Stevenson came to know the artists' haunts of Paris, Barbizon and Grèz through his cousin. Bob's great friend in Paris was his fellow student Will Low.

Various attempts have been made to identify the students who then attended Carolus-Duran's 'Atelier'. The Master began teaching only in 1872, at the request of a American art student, Robert Hinkley. Low, who joined in 1873, was thus amongst the first students, but throughput was considerable, and the identity of some of the characters is uncertain. One person who was certainly there at first was James Carrol Beckwith (1852-1917), a sort of monitor to Carolus Duran. Emile-Auguste Carolus-Duran (1838-1917) was, early on, influenced by the realism of Courbet, and it was only later in life that he became a fashionable portrait painter. He is not very highly regarded now, but his studio was looked upon as innovative in the early seventies. Partly because it was easier to get into, it was attended by young British and American students, and by students who preferred the master's unconventional approach.

In addition to Low, Wyatt Eaton (1849-1896) and Hyram Reynolds Bloomer (1845-1911), two Americans, and the mercurial Frank O'Meara (1853-1888), a young Irishman who was probably the most capable, and important painter in the group which later frequented Grèz, and was one of Carolus Duran's first pupils, were also students at the atelier then. Edward Stott (1859-1918), Lowell Birge Harrison (1854-1929), and Arthur Heseltine (1855-1830), all denizens of Grèz, and Theodore Robinson (1852-1896) and John Singer Sargent (1856-1925), both of whom were particularly friendly with RLS at different times, were students at the same studio rather later, as was Ernest Parton (1845-1933), who illustrated Bob's article about Grèz. RLS first encountered members of the group in Paris in April 1874, just before Sargent joined the atelier. Sargent was, of course, undoubtedly the most famous alumnus of Carolus Duran's. In *The Wrecker* he appears as 'Corporal John (who was already a sort of young master)'.

O'Meara provides the bridge between the Stevensons and the group of Scottish painters known as 'the Glasgow Boys', some of whom learned how to paint at Grèz-sur-Loing. Grèz, on the edge of the Forest of Fontainebleau, was where Stevenson met his wife, and where he and Bob were the centre of attention for three summers amongst the artists who frequented the place.

Perhaps the most important of the Scottish painters, although he remained on the periphery of the group rather than being a central figure, was the 'Scottish Manet', Arthur Melville (1855-1904). He was one of the most gifted Scots of his generation, and he was, perhaps, the pre-eminent 'Scottish Impressionist'. Melville attended Julien's atelier in Paris and first went to Grèz in 1878, where he encountered RLS and Fanny Osbourne. Agnes Mackay in her biography of Melville states that 'many years later he spoke of the disconcerting presence of Mrs Osbourne in the midst of this community of painters.' Melville spent much of 1879 in Grèz. Among his close friends there were 'Joe' [Arthur] Heseltine, and Middleton Jameson (d1919), a young Scottish painter who had arrived in Grèz in 1874 and was a member of the coterie which surrounded the Stevensons. However, Melville was never so closely involved with Stevenson as was Jameson who is mentioned by Birge Harrison in his account of Stevenson's time at Grèz. Notable pictures executed by Melville in Grèz include the watercolour 'The Kingcup Meadow', and the oil 'Les Laveuses', reminiscent of Lavery.

Heseltine settled in Marlotte, and stayed there for the rest of his days. Like many other painters one of his subjects was 'The Old Bridge at Grèz', but he was never one of the most significant members of this artistic community. More important was William Stott, although he was a painter who went out of fashion, and was eventually much mocked. As a younger man he was influential and provided a link between the group at Grèz, and Whistler with whom he was, at one time, very friendly. However, he fell out with the famous man who cruelly, but typically, pronounced, when Stott died on a packet boat going to Ireland, 'He died at sea, where he always was.'

William Stott of Oldham (1857-1900), so-called to distinguish him from his fellow Lancastrian, Edward Stott (who also painted at Grèz, and was a pupil of Carolus-Duran), influenced John Lavery (1856-1941), Alexander Roche (1861-1921), William Kennedy (1859-1918), and Thomas Millie Dow (1848-1919), another pupil of Carolus Duran's who was his closest friend. These four, together with Melville, were key 'Glasgow Boys', and Grèz was central to their artistic education. Bob Stevenson wrote an appreciation of Wm. Stott in *Studio* after he died:

> In the vicissitudes of its history Grèz came to be much frequented by Anglo-Saxons, and among the young men whom Mr Stott found trying to express the exquisite delicacy of the still stream, with its tall bending poplars and shimmering river growths, the most remarkable perhaps was the late Frank O'Meara. With a poetic temperament and an eye but poorly

satisfied with the result of commonplace realism. O'Meara was always meditating on the way to use the beauty of these shapely growths, these still breadths of mist-wrapped, and the soft yet decided elegance of a foreground of large-leaved riverside plants. To the expression of this scenery Mr. Stott brought a mind of more practical energy, a complete training and also a robuster constitution. He rapidly built up a style which contained the elements of this natural poetry, and the results of previous study.

In his autobiography Sir John Lavery acknowledged his debt to his fellow countryman, O'Meara – Lavery was legitimately a 'Glasgow Boy' having grown up near, and worked in the city, but he was born in Belfast. Two or three of William Stott's paintings, 'The Ferry' [1882] and 'The Bathers' [c1882], which was shown at the Glasgow Institute in 1883, clearly provided Lavery with inspiration for his notable river pictures. He once said he had painted the Bridge at Grèz at least ten times. For a long time his most famous work, originally called 'A Passing Salute', but later entitled 'The Bridge at Grèz' [1883] was unlocated, but it has recently been re-discovered and was exhibited in Edinburgh and London in 1991. Lavery told a good story about this picture which went to America. A dealer, keen to impress, said to him "I think, Sir, you are perhaps the best-known British painter whose work has reached the States. There sure is no picture more talked about than your portrait of the beautiful Irish girl, Bridget Gray."

Fernande Sadler, who wrote *L'Hôtel Chevillon et les Artistes de Grès-sur-Loing* [1938] corresponded with Lavery who responded to her warmly with his recollections of the place. He mentions three other painters, Jules Bastien-Lepage (1848-84), whom Lavery met in Paris and whose strangely lit landscapes with peasants strongly influenced 'the Glasgow Boys', Eugène Vail (b.1857), and Jean Charles Cazin (1841-1901), both landscape painters:

> Thank you for your friendly letter, I made the acquaintance of Grèz-sur-Loing through Eugène Vail. We were both at the atelier Julian and we decided to go for the week-end. I stayed nine months.

> It was the first colony of artists I was part of and I was so taken with the novelty and the beauty of the place and its inhabitants after my work in Paris that I renounced Paris and painting nudes and I became a landscape painter, influenced by Bastien Lepage and Cazin and learned to love life *en plein air* so much that Paris seemed oppressive. When I had to go

there for my to purchase art materials I would take an early morning train so that it was possible for me to return the same day. All that is now changed, I hurry back to the town from the country; the appeal of the country is short lived.

Robert Louis Stevenson had just left Grèz; his friends Frank O'Meara, Stott of Oldham, Harrison and the others told me stories of this charming personality. Your letter reminds me of names I had almost forgotten to remember. The Swedish and American elements were stronger than the British. Carl Larsson was perhaps the most interesting Swedish painter. Harrison, the American, Stott, the Englishman, and O'Meara, the Irishman, had a great deal of influence on me, above all the last of the three, during the three or four seasons I spent at Grèz. I do not remember having met a French painter, apart from Cazin who used to go to visit his brother-in-law, Arthur Heseltine. I would send you anecdotes, but my memory is such that it functions only rarely, but not to order.

In *From Grèz to Glasgow* Kenneth McConkey comments as follows about a later picture of the bridge which carries echoes of 'A Passing Salute' which is called 'Under The Cherry Tree' or 'On the Loing – An Afternoon Chat' [1884], now in the Ulster Museum, Belfast:

Here all that he had learnt from O'Meara, Stott, and Bastien-Lepage was to be utilised. He considered the angle of viewpoint, the depth of field and the staging of the motifs and their relationship to one another.

Lavery's other work executed in Grèz includes 'A Grey Summer's Day, Grèz' [1883], 'Return from Market' [c1884], 'La Laveuse' [1883] and 'The Principal Street at Grèz' [1884]. Lavery's autobiography devotes a good deal of space to Louis Weldon Hawkins (d.1910) who was there in Stevenson's time, and to Frederick Delius whom he must have met on a later visit. Delius moved to Grèz in 1897 to live with Jelka Helen von Rosen. Sadly O'Meara contracted the malaria which killed him in Grèz, which makes the mosquitoes mentioned by Lavery rather more menacing than they seem. Although it refers to a later period the passage casts interesting light on the mores of the colony of painters in the village:

One day a German girl, with the lovely name of Delka Rosen, arrived and caused some stir. Not because of her nationality – she spoke French and English without an accent – but because she had advanced ideas on art and life. She rented a large house which had not been lived in for years. Then a personality arrived: a rather delicate, sensitive young man called Delius who went to live with her quite openly, and, as a matter of course, took it for granted that young people of the opposite sex should live together if they so pleased. Later Delka became his wife. The garden which ran down from the house to the river, was completely shut in and made an ideal open air studio for models which Delka made great use of, making it a small and select nudist camp which would have been a complete success if it had not been for the mosquitoes.

Lloyd Osbourne (1868-1947), RLS's step-son, kept in touch with Grèz, revisited it several times, and stayed with Delius. He was there when war broke out in 1914.

Lavery is pre-eminent amongst the Glasgow Boys in respect of the amount of his work which can be definitely attributed to Grèz. Fernande Sadler, referred to above, who carefully examined the registers of the Hôtel Chevillon, asserts that James Guthrie visited Grèz with his 'inseparable friend', Lavery, but this was almost certainly Kennedy and not Guthrie.

Bridge at Grèz: the bridge over the Loing with its prominent starlings, the subject of numerous paintings by many artists including Lavery

Guthrie was dissuaded from studying in France, although he went to Paris and was surely influenced by Courbet and by Bastien Lepage.

William Kennedy was a close friend of Lavery, who trained with Bastien Lepage and others in Paris. He was in Fontainebleau in 1881, went to Grèz in 1882, and painted children playing in the village street. He was in Grèz in both of the following years, showing his work in Paisley and in Glasgow. Much of this is unlocated, but an important canvas, 'Spring' [1884], is in Renfrew District Museum and Art Gallery. Roger Billcliffe in his book *The Glasgow Boys* suggests that the influence of Thomas Millie Dow's sojourn in Grèz can be seen in paintings which he executed in America. Dow was very friendly with William Stott, who painted his portrait when he was in Grèz. It is known that Roche visited Grèz, but little of his early work has been described, and none that can be definitely attributed to the period when he there. It can also be noted here that much later, in 1896, another painter of the Glasgow School, David Gauld (1865-1936), went to Grèz, and executed a significant series of landscapes there.

This charming French village was central to the development of some of the Glasgow Boys at the same time as Stevenson was painting word pictures of the place in the *Magazine of Art*, and elsewhere. It would be idle to pretend that the écrivain écossais was central to developments at Grèz, but he contributed significantly to artistic life there, and experienced it to the full. He did not see the 'Black Cat' after it became established as a night club, nor was he in Glasgow to see the pictures of Grèz which the 'Glasgow Boys' exhibited, but he was in France when it mattered.

Menton: an artist's impression of C19 Menton

Stevenson in France: Menton

> By a curious irony of fate, the places to which we are sent when health deserts us are often singularly beautiful.
>
> [R.L. Stevenson *Ordered South*]

> Everything in this favoured locality is suited to the requirements of invalids and persons of delicate constitution. The climate is perhaps the mildest upon the entire coast. Nowhere on the northern Mediterranean shore does the lemon tree grow with equal luxuriance. Fogs and dews are unknown, the sky is cloudless; the town is so encircled by mountains that the mistral is scarcely ever felt, and the temperature scarcely ever falls below freezing point. According to Dr Henry J. Bennet, an English physician who may be said to have discovered Menton thirty years ago (monument in the Rue Partouneaux), persons affected with pulmonory disease, either in the first or second stages, derive great benefit from passing the winter there. [Cook's *Traveller's Handbook* 1912]

Stevenson knew the Riviera before it was 'The Riviera'. He was taken to Menton as a boy in early 1863, shortly after the district had been acquired by France. The railway had not reached Menton, and the spectacular modern resorts of the 'Côte d'Azur' were still, by and large, overgrown villages. The eastern part of Menton was scarcely developed.

In relation to Stevenson's life, Menton is particularly significant in two ways. First of all he was taken there twice as a child – he returned to the

Menton: the Jardin Biovès

resort in the winter of 1863/4 – and it was where he first gained a knowledge of France, and of things French. Secondly it was where he first went when, in 1873/4, he travelled abroad by himself as a young man. A shrewd doctor recognised that it might well be beneficial to his health to be separated from his parents, and Menton inspired one of his first independently published pieces of work, the essay *Ordered South.*

We have a detailed account of his first sojourn in a diary kept by his nurse Alison Cunningham [*Cummy's Diary*, edited by R.T. Skinner]. The occasion for going there in the first instance was his mother's ill-health which continued to cause sufficient concern for them to return the following winter. RLS was left at a boarding school in England during the autumn term, but he was unhappy there, and his father took him out to Menton before Christmas. Little is known about that second visit. He was fourteen years of age, and it can be assumed that it was an 'action replay' of the first visit: having a tutor, going for walks and socialising. Boys of thirteen and fourteen are usually both perceptive and receptive, and he probably considered that he became familiar with the geography of Menton at that time. He thought of Menton when a boyhood friend of his died as a comparatively young man. In certain weather conditions the hills of Corsica can be seen from Menton. To RLS his friend James Ferrier was 'a vision, like Corsica from the Corniche.'

When he went there in 1873 he stayed, first of all, at the Hôtel du Pavillon, then an isolated building situated on the dunes of the west bay towards Cap-Martin. It is opposite the Palais Carnolès, the former villa residence of the Princes of Monaco. It served formerly as a barracks for the Prince's military retinue; hence its name. The hotel is still there, now called Hôtel Prince des Galles, almost lost in a crowd of other hotels. This is a reminder of what an 'English' (or, more correctly, British) resort Menton was. In the winter of 1863/4 Thomas Stevenson was a member of the Committee for the celebrations held to mark the wedding of the Prince of Wales. Queen Victoria stayed in Menton in 1882, and there is a statue of her there. Edward himself,

Hôtel Prince de Galles, formerly the Hôtel du Pavillon

29

it is reported, tended to stay on the Royal Yacht when his mother was in town.

RLS's first letter home in 1873, written to his mother on his birthday, harks back to the boyhood visits. Menton is situated where three mountain torrents – the Carei (the stream which waters the splendid Jardin Biovès), the Borrigo and the Gorbio – tumbled into the sea during the winter months. The Villa Bosano where the family stayed at first in 1863 was near the Gorbio. He mentions the new railway, which had arrived in 1868, and was carried on viaducts over the torrents, past 'the bone caves' [Bassi Roussi] which were thought in Stevenson's day to have provided a skull of the missing link ['Menton Man']. 'The old Chapel... at the entrance to the Gorbio valley,' he reported, 'is now entirely submerged under a shining new villa...' He referred, too, to the terraced Vieux cimetière above the town, and to the recently erected 'Princess Eugenie Jetty'. In his next letter he describes 'a coign of vantage', probably a little way up the Gorbio, to Fanny Sitwell 'where one has a fair view down the valley and on to the blue floor of the sea'.

RLS was a hesitant poet, and he kept his poems to himself for a long time, but the following poem, dated 7th December, and almost certainly composed with Fanny Sitwell, with whom he was infatuated, in mind, was eventually published in 1916:

Hôtel Prince de Galles

Swallows travel to and fro,
And the great winds come and go,
And the steady breezes blow,
Bearing perfume, bearing love.
Breezes hasten, swallows fly,
Towered clouds forever ply,
And at noonday you and I
See the same sun shine above.

Dew and rain fall everywhere,
Harvests ripen, flowers are fair,
And the whole round earth is bare
To the moonshine and the sun;
And the live air fanned with wings,
Bright with breeze and sunshine brings
Into contact distant things,
And makes all the countries one.

Let us wander where we will,
Something kindred greets us still;
Something seen on vale or hill
Falls familiar on the heart;
So, at scent or sound, or sight,
Severed souls by day and night
Tremble with the same delight –
Tremble, half the world apart.

His enthusiasm for Menton is very marked. He is full of delight in its sights, its sounds and its smells. 'Is the sky blue?' he asks Charles Baxter, 'You poor critter, you never saw blue sky worth being called blue in the same day with it.'

From Menton he said that he visited Dr Bennet in Nice, and reported himself exhausted, unable to remember French. At Christmas Sidney Colvin came to see him and 'found him without tangible disease, but very weak and ailing'.

James Henry Bennet MD (1816-1891) was born in Manchester, but was educated in Paris. His father was the inventor of corduroy. He practised in Menton from 1869 until his death from tuberculosis. He specialised in the treatment of consumption by climatic means, and, as early as 1861, he had published *Mentone and the Riviera as a Winter Climate*. Wm. Miller who wintered in Menton in 1876/7 and 1877/8 stated that Bennet took quarters in the Hôtel des Anglais opposite the bathing establishment on the East Bay. Stevenson reports visiting Bennet in Nice, which suggests that he may have lived there.

RLS and Colvin went to Monaco and Monte Carlo before returning, early in January, to the Hotel Mirabeau at the eastern end of Menton. At Monte Carlo RLS and his friend Colvin were in sufficiently high spirits to devise an amusing spoof of the advertisements produced by Continental hotels, foreshadowing much humour of the same sort. Stevenson, at least, already had a great deal of experience of such hotels. His French biographer, Carré, calls the language 'kitchen French':

GRAND HOTEL GODAM
(Englisch-House)
PLACE DU PARADIS-ALCIBIADE KROMESKY,
PROPRIÉTAIRE

'Tous les agréments du *Hihg-Life* se trouvent réunis dans ce magnifique établissement, nouvellement organisé et entretenu sur le pied confortable le plus recherché. – Salons de Societé, de Lecture et de Billiard.'

'Pension à prix modérés. Cuisine et service hors ligne. Spécialités de rosbif, rhum, thé Pekoé, porterbeer, wischky, old Thom et autre consommations dans le goût britannique. – On parle toutes les langues.'

THE GREAT GOD-DAMN HOTEL
PLACE DU PARADIS-ALCIBIADES KROMESKY,
PROPRIETAR

'All the agreements of hihg-life are reunited in this magnificent establishment, newly organised, and entertained upon the footing of the most researchd confortable. – Salons of Society, Lecture, and Billiard.'

'Pension to moderate prices. Kitchen and service out of common. Specialitys of roasbeef, rhum-punsch, Pekoë tea, porterbeer, wischkey, old Thom, and other consummations in the britisch taste. – One speaks all the languages.'

At the Mirabeau the company seemed more congenial, and RLS prospered. In a later letter home he says that his French accent has been admired, and that he has been speaking the language all day. At the Mirabeau he found himself in the company of two aristocratic Russian women, the Russian aristocracy making as much use of the resort as did the British, an American family, and a companionable French painter called Robinet. The relationships which he established there were important: they were independent relationships, the first which had arisen, including that with Fanny Sitwell and Sidney Colvin, independent of his family network. He wondered, in letters to Fanny Sitwell, whether one of the women was trying to seduce him, and he became enchanted with a child who could speak half a dozen languages. RLS grew up in Menton.

In February, 1874 he wrote a poem, *To Mesdames Zassetsky and Garshine*, in Lallans, dedicated to his two Russian friends, which captures the warmth of Menton and the warmth of their friendship:

> – Sic neuk beside the southern sea
> I soucht – sic place o' quiet lee
> Frae a' the winds o' life. To me,
> Fate, rarely fair,
> Had set a freendly company
> To meet me there.
>
> Kindly by them they gart me sit,
> An' blythe was I to bide a bit.
> Licht as o' some hame fireside lit
> My life for me.
> – Ower early maun I rise an' quit
> This happy lee.

Nowadays Menton rightly makes a fuss of Jean Cocteau (1889-1963), the literary and artistic polymath who has a museum, and of Katherine Mansfield [Kathleen Beauchamp, then Kathleen Middleton Murray] (1888-1923), the short story-writer, who came to Menton for her health at the end of her life. There is a statue, too, to the American poet, Henry Wadsworth Longfellow (1807-82) who visited Menton. The *Blue Guide* mentions Stevenson together with the inadvertent founder of Rugby Football, William Webb Ellis, the British historian, John Richard Green (1837-83), the Spanish novelist Vincente Ibánez (1867-1928), author of *Blood and Sand*, sometimes called the 'Spanish Zola', and the distinguished Irish poet, W.B. Yeats (1865-1939) who spent 1937/8 in Menton before dying at Cap Martin. It can be noted that while Stevenson, like the others, did come as an invalid, unlike the others, he came when he was young, and Menton thus exercised a formative influence on him.

In addition to these literary associations, there was an important literary encounter which is less well remembered in Menton, but which is of particular interest in connection with Stevenson. The prolific Scottish man-of-letters, Andrew Lang (1844-1912), then an Oxford don having been elected to a fellowship at Merton in 1868, was taken ill, and ordered to take a complete rest in the autumn of 1872. The following winter, too, he was in Menton, and it appears to have cleared up his lung trouble. He was, early on, a poet and had, in 1872, published *Rhymes and Ballads of Old France*, consisting of some poems of his own together with translations of Villon, Ronsard, Charles of Orleans, Hugo and others. He was, in many ways, very like Stevenson in appearance; both went to Edinburgh Academy, and both knew the Sellars in Edinburgh. However, they had not met, and were introduced in Menton. Neither particularly liked the other at first, but they quickly discovered that they had much in common, and a lifelong literary friendship was established. At the very end of Stevenson's life they collaborated, half a world apart, in a novel, *The Young Chevalier* which was begun by Stevenson, and had its first setting in Avignon. Lang is remembered as a folklorist, a translator, and a notable editor. However, he was very significant as a journalist who promoted many writers, including Stevenson, whose work he undoubtedly helped to bring to a wide public.

We have several accounts of their meeting. RLS's friend Colvin was also his literary mentor, and he perceived Lang as an important contact for the young Stevenson. However, he was not very sanguine about introducing them:

> It was not without some trepidation that I first brought them together in those Mentone days, for I suppose no two young Scots, especially no two sharing so many literary tastes, were ever more unlike by temperament and training. On the one hand the young Oxford don, a successful and typical scholar on the regular academic lines, picturesque by the gift of nature, but fastidiously correct and reserved, purely English in speech, with a recurring falsetto note in the voice – that kind of falsetto which bespeaks of langour rather than vehemence; full of literature and pleasantry, but on his guard, even to affectation against any show of emotion, and constantly dissembling the perfervidum ingenium of his race, if he had it, under a cloak of indifference and light banter. On the other hand, the brilliant irregularly educated lad from Edinburgh, to the conventional eye an eccentrically ill-clad and long-haired nondescript, with

the rich Lallan accent on his tongue, the obvious innate virility and spirit of adventure in him ever in mutiny against invalid habits imposed by ill-health, the vivid, demonstrative ways, every impulse of his heart and mind flashing out in the play of eye, feature and gesture, no less than in the humorous riot and poetical abundance of his talk. [Colvin *Memories and Notes* 1921]

Lang later gave Clayton Hamilton a staccato account of the meeting, but he left it in writing in *Adventures Among Books*:

He looked, as in my eyes he always did look, more like a lass than a lad, with a rather long, smooth oval face, brown hair worn at greater length than is common, large lucid eyes...His colour was a trifle hectic, as is not unusual at Mentone, but he seemed, under his big blue cloak, to be of slender, yet agile frame. He was like nobody else whom I ever met. There was a sort of uncommon celerity in changing expression in thought and speech. His cloak and Tyrolese (he would admit the innocent impeachment) were decidedly dear to him.

Ordered South is considered to be a mature piece for such a young writer as Stevenson was. Colvin has pointed out that, in spite of his prolonged illnesses, it was one of the few things he ever wrote from the point of view of an invalid.

There is more than a hint of Menton, too in *Health and Mountains* and of the time Stevenson spent there in 1873/4. It is necessary to remember that he was out of sorts at the time, and that, elsewhere, he is much kinder to Menton than in this passage:

A year or two ago and the wounded soldiery of mankind were all shut up together in some basking angle of the Riviera, walking a dusty promenade or sitting in dusty olive-yards within earshot of interminable and unchanging surf – idle among spiritless idlers; not perhaps dying, yet hardly living either, and aspiring, sometimes fiercely, after livelier weather and some vivifying change. These were certainly beautiful places to live in, and the climate was wooing in its softness. Yet there was a later shiver in the sunshine; you were not certain whether you were being wooed; and these mild shores would sometimes seem to you to be the shores of death. There was a lack of a manly element; the air was not reactive;

> you might write bits of poetry and practise resignation, but
> you did not feel that here was a good spot to repair your
> tissue or regain your nerve. [*Health and Mountains*]

The dusty promenades were soon paved over, but that, too, brought complaints from hard-to-please British literary visitors like Augustus Hare (1834-1903) who, in 1890, complained about the paved walks and 'hideous stuccoed villas in the worst taste'. Hare has, however, been criticised as the most boring of all authors. A more harmonious, if intriguing, note is struck by Andrew Lang, writing to Stevenson at the beginning of their friendship:

> "Nothing in particular happened after you left Mentone – A
> scandal or two – but only the minor commandments were
> infringed..."

Stevenson in France:
The Latin Quarter

RLS was twenty-three years old when he first visited Paris as a young man, and met some of his cousin Bob's artist friends in April 1874. He had just been in Menton recovering from a bout of ill-health. It was his firm intention to be a writer, and to him Paris was a source of copy, a source of books, and a place where he could learn to write. It was also a place for him to grow up. For the next five years he went to Paris whenever he could, and it was in France that he met and fell in love with Fanny Osbourne whom he was to follow to the United States and marry:

> There was no year from 1874 to 1879 in which he did not pay one or more visits of several weeks duration to another part of France. Except for the time that he was in the Cévennes and on his cruise down the Oise, he stayed mostly on the outskirts of the forest of Fontainebleau, or in Paris itself. Sometimes, as at Monastier, he was alone; sometimes, as at Nemours or at Cernay-la-Ville, he was with his cousin Bob or Sir Walter Simpson; but for the most part he lived in familiar intercourse with the artists who frequented his favourite resorts. The life was congenial to him, and his companions understood his temperament, if they did not necessarily appreciate his passion for letters. [Graham Balfour]

R.A.M. Stevenson is now a somewhat shadowy figure, an important 'extra' in the cast of characters who appear in the life story of the famous Scottish author, it is true, but much less substantial in his own right. Both Robert

Alan, and Robert Louis Stevenson were called Robert after their grandfather, the famous Scottish engineer, Robert Stevenson. Because R.A.M. Stevenson was the older of the two it was he who, in the Stevenson family, was known as 'Bob', whereas R.L.S. was known as 'Lewis', or, as he affected to spell it, 'Louis'. As the older of the two Bob was the more influential when they were boys; indeed he was, at one time, considered by RLS's parents to be a bad influence on him. In his late twenties Bob Stevenson was tall and handsome, somewhat southern European in appearance, Spanish or Mexican perhaps, with a fashionable moustache. This dashing man was admired by everyone who met him in his youth. 'In our dissonant orchestra,' wrote Will Low, 'the baton of leader was in the hands of the elder of the two cousins.'

R.A.M. Stevenson: portrait by Krøyer

Will H. Low's book *A Chronicle of Friendships* is the most important source of information about the Stevensons' days in Paris, indeed it is a very significant source of information about life in the Latin Quarter during that period generally. William Hicock Low (1853-1932) was a young American painter who came to study in Paris in 1873. He later married a Frenchwoman, and went to live in Montigny on the banks of the Loing. He was thus an inside observer of artistic life both in Paris, and on the skirts of the Forest of Fontainebleau which, for a period, was dominated by the two Stevensons. Low and Bob Stevenson became close friends in Paris in 1873/4. Louis Stevenson therefore had ready made access to the *Scènes de la Vie de Bohème*, fashionably chronicled by Henri Murger (1822-61) in 1848, and to the city brilliantly evoked by Honoré de Balzac (1799-1850). The narrator in *The Wrecker* is an American art student, partly based on Low, and partly on an American sculptor, but the sentiments he sometimes expresses are just as much Stevenson's. Here he describes his reactions to Paris:

> Every man has his own romance; mine clustered exclusively about the practice of the arts, the life of the Latin Quarter students, and the world of Paris as depicted by that grimy wizard, the author of the *Comédie Humaine*. I was not disappointed – I could not have been; for I did not see the facts, I brought them with me ready made...
>
> At this time we were all a little Murger-mad in the Latin Quarter. The play of the *Vie de Bohème* (a dreary snivelling piece) had been produced at the Odéon, had run an unconscionable time – for Paris – and revived the freshness of the legend. The same business, you may say, or there and thereabout, was being privately enacted in consequence in every garret in the neighbourhood, and a good third of the students were consciously impersonating Rodolphe or Schaunard, to their own incommunicable satisfaction. Some of us went far, and some farther. I always looked with awful envy (for instance) on a certain countryman of my own who had a studio in the Rue Monsieur le Prince, wore boots, and long hair in a net, and could be seen tramping off, in this guise, to the worst eating-house of the quarter, followed by a Corsican model, his mistress, in the conspicuous costume of her race and calling.
> [*The Wrecker*]

In the late C19 Paris was described as the Capital of Art and then, as now, Montmartre was probably the part of the city most associated in the public

212, PARIS — Boulevard Montmartre   E. L. D.

Montmartre

mind with the arts, but the Left Bank was almost equally significant, if not more significant so far as Fine Art was concerned. This was where the Latin Quarter was, bounded by the Boulevard St Michel and the Boulevard Montparnasse. Modern Paris was being built and rebuilt then. If it was not entirely rural Montmartre was semi-rural, just being developed; the Sacré Cœur was begun in 1876 and only finished in 1912. Not long before Baron Haussmann had created the fine boulevards which still distinguish the city, and had broken through the network of old streets, some of which were blocked off. As a consequence of the Siege of Paris, and the Commune, public buildings – including a part of the Louvre and the Tuileries Palace – had been burned down, and trees cut for firewood. Nowadays, the scenes which Stevenson saw have to be imagined, but the Latin Quarter still retains some of its character.

'L'Atelier des Elèves de Monsieur Carolus-Duran' was situated at 81 Boulevard Montparnasse. It was entered from a alleyway called the Passage Stanislaus, and was a block of studios built around a courtyard which housed thirty or forty artists and art students:

> The rooms were lofty, a huge window occupying the whole
> of one side about ten feet above the floor, and, opposite, at
> the same height, a platform projected seven or eight feet into
> the studio, which, reached by a ladder, served as a bed
> chamber for the bachelor occupant. I have even seen efforts

at a ménage established on these lofty perches, but these
unions were frowned on by our landlady; for Madame la
Propriétaire ruled her sometimes unruly tenants with a rod
of iron... [Will H. Low *A Chronicle of Friendships*]

The studios on the ground floor were, sensibly enough, occupied by
sculptors, those above by painters. At the end of the courtyard furthest
from the entrance the Proprietrix lived on two floors, and above this was
a larger studio where the 'Atelier' was held. Low describes a 'small detached
building' on the righthand side of the entrance to the courtyard the ground
floor of which was the office of the concierge, and above which were two
further studios, one large, with a separate bedroom and kitchen, the other
very small in which a large cupboard served as a bedroom. Bob Stevenson
occupied the larger of these two, and was often visited there by RLS.

By far the best description of these studios comes in Low's book, a
description on which many subsequent studies have relied. However,
Stevenson himself has left some record of them in *A Studio of Ladies*. It
is an account in which his gentle irony distinguishes it as one of his pieces:

Students of Art in Paris are usually attached to some painter
of name, in whose wake they humbly follow. The master
gives them so much of his time for criticism and advice, and
when he is occupied on a work of any magnitude, employs

Moulin Rouge

41

the most capable to lay it in. The pupils pay by subscription for the models and the large studio in which they work. Some learn to forge the master's touch with great nicety; others recoil to the opposite, and take pleasure in producing battle-pieces under the tuition of a painter of sheep; but all, when they come to exhibit in the Salon, sign themselves as the pupil of M. Couture, or M. Gérome or M. Carolus-Duran, as the case may be. This is an arrangement honourable and useful to both parties.

Further on he reports on the advantage enjoyed by these residents and the way in which non-residents overcame it. He calls his friend from Grèz, Frank O'Meara, 'Shaun O'Shaughnessy':

Monday morning is an epoch in studio existence; it is then that a new model begins a sitting, and those that arrive first have first choice of places for the week. At Carolus-Duran's, the other year, there were one or two fellows who lived in the same building with the studio. These would arise wilily at three or four on Monday morning, and, after having inscribed their names upon the board, return cozily to roost. You may imagine the discomfiture of early students from all parts of Paris, when they dropped in as soon as the studio was opened, and found a whole company of names already registered. At last the trick got wind. The porter was found to be venal; through his connivance Shaun O'Shaughnessy and the whole ruck of out-students made their entrance on Sunday evening; and when their tricksy comrades crept down before daybreak with a bit of candle and their finger to their nose, they found the tables turned, and had to inscribe themselves humbly in the fag-end of the class. [*A Studio of Ladies*]

81, Boulevard Montparnasse was situated close to the church of Notre Dame des Champs, then being built, and the Gare Montparnasse, the station of the Western Railway. On the opposite side of the road where the Rue de Rennes approaches the station, at 1, Avenue du Départ was Lavenue's, the fashionable restaurant where, when they were in funds, the young artists dined, and set the world to rights. Not very far in the opposite direction was the most attractive of public parks in Paris the Luxembourg Gardens:

It is a garden I have always loved. You sit there in a public place of history and fiction. Barras and Fouché have looked from these windows. Lousteau and De Banville (one as real as the other) have rhymed upon these benches. The city tramples by without the railings to lively measure; and within and about you, trees rustle, children and sparrows utter their small cries and the statues look on for ever. [*The Wrecker*]

The gardens also feature in a letter quoted by Balfour which gives an idea of the way in which they spent much of their time. It also contains a reference to one of Low's closest French friends the sculptor Adrien-Etienne Gaudez (1845-1902):

> Yesterday I had a splendid day. Luxembourg in the morning. Breakfast. Bob, Gaudez, the sculptor, Low and I: hours of very good talk in the French idiom. All afternoon in the Louvre, till they turned us out unwilling. At night, the Français, *Rome Vaincue*, an impossible play, with Sarah Bernhart as the blind grandmother.

Between Carolus Duran's and the Luxembourg Gardens, R. Notre Dame des Champs connects Bvd. Montparnasse with R. de Rennes. This street was the heart of the artists' quarter with more studios than any other in Paris.

Carolus Duran's own studio was at 58, Rue Notre Dame des Champs; Rosa Bonheur had a studio at No 61; at No 75 was the huge studio of Adolphe William Bouguereau (1825-1905), who was a Member of the Academy of Beaux Arts, and a tutor at Julian's Atelier; at No 86 Whistler occupied a studio at one time; and so on. Perhaps the most famous apartment in the street was that occupied by George du Maurier and his artist friends at No 53 Rue Notre Dame des Champs in 1856. Du Maurier made the apartment central to his notorious novel *Trilby* in which his portrait of Whistler as the king of 'Bohemia' greatly offended the artist who, in 1856/7 had almost taken a share in the studio, and was a frequent visitor to it. Twenty years later Beckwith took on a similar large apartment at No 73 bis which was later shared by Sargent, and eventually occupied by Sargent alone. One of Sargent's biographers describes the situation, providing a strong link with Stevenson through O'Meara and Robinson, and Fanny and Isobel Osbourne:

> As winter came on, the members of the Carolus Duran atelier drifted back to Paris from their haunts at Grèz, Fontainebleau, and Brittany. Beckwith rather optimistically took a large studio on the fifth floor of a building only four or five blocks from the Duran atelier, which was to cost him a thousand francs

a year. How he ever hoped to meet such a rental is difficult to imagine, and soon the immensity of it struck him too, for he was asking his friends to come and work there with him, to help pay the rent. At different times, and often together, Frank Fowler, George Becker, Theodore Robinson, and Fanny and Isobel Osbourne, shared it with him. [Charles Merill Mount *John Singer Sargent* 1957]

We do not learn about this from either Fanny or Isobel Osbourne. Fanny Osbourne (1840-1914), was ten years older than Stevenson, and estranged from her husband, trying to make her way on the Continent with three children, Isobel, aged sixteen, Lloyd, eight, and Harvey, four. When they arrived in Paris in the sad winter 1875/76 during which Fanny's younger son eventually died, they had an apartment in the Rue de Naples, near the Gare St Lazare, and their artistic life was based on the artists' quarters North of the Seine. While Fanny nursed her child, Belle was enrolled at the Académie Julian's 'Atelier des Dames' in an alley off the Boulevard d'Italiens:

It was an unheard of thing to allow a young girl of sixteen to walk alone in Paris; she must at least have a maid in attendance. I went by myself to the studio every morning and had many adventures. [*This Life I've Loved*]

Belle was clearly a very attractive young woman, and not without talent as an art student. Her teacher was Tony Robert-Fleury and, as Belle pointed out in her autobiography he was brutally frank, as he was with her, only with students who showed promise. He and Bouguereau were Julian's two principal teachers. We know a good deal about the Academy Julian which was one of the most popular in Paris. One of the reasons why it was so successful was because it admitted women, and was attended when Belle was there, among many others, by Maria Konstantinowna Bashkirtseff (1860-1884), towards whom Fleury was particularly attentive, who kept a detailed journal which created a sensation when it was published, and by George Moore (1852-1933), the Irish novelist and poet, another literary man amongst artists, who wrote *Confessions of a Young Man* which provides another graphic account of student life in Paris at the time. Belle seems to have attended the 'Atelier des Dames', for women only, while the other two were in a mixed studio, but the teaching staff seem to have been the same.

In early 1877 Stevenson wrote the piece for *London* called 'A Studio of Ladies'. Stevenson's description of Julian, and of the women who attended the studio was not kind, but probably quite justified:

M. Concert, a heavy shouldered French painter, with a sneering countenance, a long nose, and a most seductive deportment, had thrown open his atelier to ladies, and pocketed their money with great sweetness. To him flocked quite a troop of English, Americans, and French, and a knot of indefatigable Swedes.

He goes on to describe the women's conversation, and then the way in which they, the Swedes in particular, were singularly hard on male models.

During their first winter in Paris one of the few people the Osbournes seemed to know at all well was an American sculptor who had the distinctive, French-sounding name, Pardessus. It was he who recommended Grèz to Fanny Osbourne, and it was he who was, in part, the model for Loudon Dodd in *The Wrecker* as he had been sent to Paris to learn sculpture so that his father could give him commissions in the small-town where his wealth gave him access to public office.

The following winter [76/77] Fanny took an apartment in the Rue Douai, where Belle's teacher, Robert-Fleury, had his studio. Belle mentions exploring Paris at the weekends, and sometimes during the week, with O'Meara, but not very much about going to Montparnasse. The next year they migrated even further into Montmartre, and lived in the Rue Ravignan. RLS visited both of these apartments, and there has, of course, been much speculation about the extent to which he and Fanny Osbourne were lovers then. It was Louis Stevenson's frequent journeys from Montparnasse to the 'terra incognita' of Montmartre that alerted Low to an affair. "Bob and I both recognised," he wrote, "how serious a passion held him, all impossible of realisation as it then appeared to be." Belle, in later life, suggests, probably tendentiously, that their opportunities were somewhat restricted:

> Our apartments always consisted of a sitting room where Sammy [Lloyd Osbourne] slept on a couch when he was home from school, a tiny kitchen, and an ample bedroom with two single beds for my mother and me. There was no deviation at any time from the room that I occupied with my mother.

And again, defending the family escutcheon:

> My mother constantly carried the dread that some silly canard would get back to Oakland, where any tarradiddle would make a juicy topic of conversation, and where it would reach the ears of Sam Osbourne. So as Louis's visits became more frequent and he became an acknowledged suitor, I was thrown into the role of my mother's constant chaperone.

From Sargent's biographers we get a slightly different picture. It was the eminently capable, if disconcertingly aloof, Sargent who, that same winter, painted a head of Frank O'Meara which Belle Osbourne eventually took with her to the United States, as a memento of their affair. The other affair is also said to have impressed itself on those present:

> Louis Stevenson, now a member of the Edinburgh bar, was in Paris that winter, and could be found regularly at Beckwith's. The actual state of affairs was first known to a little group in the studio, who, as the winter progressed, saw signs of affection between Louis and Fanny Osbourne grow into something more lasting.

Belle, who is not entirely reliable, refers to attending a fancy dress party in Montparnasse held in a studio belonging to H.R. Bloomer, which she further states used to belong to Du Maurier, and would therefore have been the setting for *Trilby*. This would be the studio situated at 53 Rue Notre Dame des Champs, rather than Beckwith's apartment at 73 bis, although there were changes in street numbers. Stevenson used the same party as the basis for an article in *London* which Henley dismissed as effete, but which reads today as an interesting period piece describing the atmosphere very well. He also described this night out in a letter home:

> I was out last night at a party in a fellow's studio over in Rue Notre Dame des Champs. Some of the people were in costume. One girl was so pretty and looked so happy that it did your heart good to see her. The studio looked very strange, lit with Chinese lanterns and a couple of strange lamps. The floor had been rubbed with candles and was very slippery. O'Meara, in his character of young Donnybrook, tumbled about like a pair of old boots, and —, for all he is so little, managed to fall into the arms of every girl he danced with, as he went round in the last figure of the quadrille. There was nothing to eat but sweet biscuits and nothing to drink but syrup and water. It was a rum event.

Low mentions Stevenson's disapproval of syrup and water, a subject which he touches on with feeling both in the letter and in the article. The article begins with a description of the entrance to the studio:

> Mr Elsinare's studio lies in a long, rambling silent street not a hundred miles away from the Boulevard Mont-parnasse – a quarter of Paris which is cheap, airy and free from the

visitation of tourists. The house presents to the thoroughfare a modest gable, a rickety carriage gate, and a sort of cottage on the other side of it, which looks as if was meant for the porter. The wicket stands open as we arrive, but there is no sign of life. We venture in, as we might venture after nightfall into a farm-steading, with a kind of beware-of-the-dog feeling at heart. The court is long and narrow like a bit of a country lane; the ground descends, the pavement is of the roughest; and the ladies with high heels, on their way to Mr Elsinare's, stumble in the darkness over all manner of heights and hollows, and have to pilot their drapery through many dangers.

RLS goes on to describe some of the people present. The characters have been identified as H.R. Bloomer (Smiler), Sir Walter Simpson (Willie MacIntyre), Frank O'Meara (Shaun O'Shaughnessy), and Belle Osbourne (Belle Bird). However, Simpson was not a painter who spent the winters at Grèz, and there may be something of either William Simpson, Sir Walter's brother (a suggestion made by Furnas), or even Middleton Jamieson, who was also rich, but did not have the necessary dog, in the character. Sargent told Balfour that he never knew Stevenson in France, but it is tempting to identify Mr Elsinare as Sargent:

The company is mixed as to nationality, and varied in attire. The chaperon is an Austrian Countess, who seems to have had all the Austria taken out of her by a prolonged sojourn in New York. There are many Americans, a sprinkling of French, a Swede, and some Britishers. Most of the men are in evening dress, and one or two in costume. Elsinare appears as Hamlet, and makes a very graceful host. Dear Smiler, the best of men has waxed his moustaches until he is very nearly off the face of the earth, and radiates welcome and good happiness as though he had six thousand a year and an island in the Aegean. The floor is just a trifle too much waxed for his free Californian style of dancing; and, as he goes round in the last figure of the quadrille, he falls into the arms of all the ladies in succession. It makes no difference, however, for they are mostly bigger than he is, and he carries it off with a good humour which is more beautiful than grace. Shaun O'Shaughnessy also bite the dust repeatedly with true Hibernian aplomb. George Rowland, dressed as a Yorkshire farmer of the old school, makes his entrance in character, to the unfeigned alarm of all the French. They evidently think the scalping is going to begin. But it is just Rowland's way, and they are reassured by the laughter of the rest. Willie MacIntyre, in the national costume, brings with him a powerful atmosphere of sporran. He does not dance from motives of delicacy, and tries as far as possible to keep the sporran in unfrequented corners. A sporran, like a bag-pipe, is most agreeable in the extreme distance, and in breezy, mountainous places.

The heroine of Stevenson's little piece is Belle whose qualities are effusively described. Fanny Osbourne mentions this in a letter home as if she were both flattered and perhaps aggravated by it. Belle affords us another picture of the young author in Paris:

It was while we were in Paris that Louis came bounding up the four flights of slippery waxed stairs to our flat, waving a magazine. My mother and I had just returned from the studio, O'Meara was waiting to take me out to dinner, and Mrs Wright and Marion had dropped in on the way to their rooms, so it was to a group of very interested admirers that Louis read a review of his work. It was very favourable and readers were advised to keep an eye on a rising young author, referred to as "One Stevenson." Of course that was what we called him for months.

In the Spring of 1878 Stevenson wrote, 'I am getting a lot of work ready in my mind, and as soon as I am able to square my elbows, I shall put it through my hands rapidly.' In practice 1878 turned out to be a particularly productive year, and it was a year in which he spent a very great deal of time in France, but Paris itself was not a place which featured very much in his work, and he occasionally bemoaned his lack of literary productivity there. However, there is no doubt that he reflected a great deal about what he intended to write, and that he learned how to write during this period. He mentions buying armfuls of books, going to libraries (where officials frustrated him), and to the theatre. Low describes him at work:

Louis was still a frequent visitor at "eighty-one", where I had retained my studio, and he at this time was making an excursion into journalism for a short-lived journal entitled "London". I can see him now, his lank form comfortably distributed between two chairs, industriously writing an article on – of all things in the world – the Paris Bourse.

The piece about the Bourse, like the piece about the Fancy Dress Party and the Studio of Ladies, has been re-published, and perhaps fifteen other minor articles in *London* have been attributed to him. He also wrote more important early stories and essays for this Journal. This would represent a great deal of minor work, but, except in *The Wrecker* Paris does not really survive in the way that, say, Grèz does, in his literary output.

His life in Paris is reported, as one might expect, as being characterised by episodes in restaurants, and at the theatre with his friends. Furnas, his biographer, hints that it would be interesting to know whether he was successful in the pursuit of 'that extinct mammal the grisette', or if he did pursue them, other than in his imagination. He has the hero in *The Wrecker* engage in the chase.

Stevenson was very interested in French Politics – both Béranger and Villon appealed to him because they were literary figures involved in politics – and he wrote several letters about the tension surrounding the regime of France's Soldier-President, the De Gaulle of his day, MacMahon, one of which was to a Japanese civil engineer he had met in Edinburgh:

> In France you will doubtless have heard that Marshal President MacMahon has discharged the Republican ministry, dissolved the Chamber, and put in a tag-rag ministry of his own, all pointing towards the recall of the Bonapartes, and all executed with circumstances of small tyranny and sublime stupidity which made it more irritating to the country. His popularity seems quite extinct. There was a review the other day while I was in Paris, and scarcely a cheer was given him by the people. [Letter to Kingero Fugicura 25 July 1877]

In October 1877 he wrote two letters home from Paris about the elections which were taking place:

> The elections are coming on and Paris is full of the strangest manifestos from this or the other candidate...It is altogether a curious spectacle for an Englishman; and most curious of all, the troops are pouring in hour by hour, drums beating and the tricolor at a bayonet end, to protect the freedom of elections. Is it not a strange land and a strange state of society?

The first of the letters was written from Lavenue's, but he asked for his allowance to be sent the Rue Ravignan. It was then that Fanny took Louis into her apartment to nurse an eye infection, and, not long afterwards, his illness meant that they had to return to England, where Fanny met some of his English friends. From Edinburgh he wrote a further letter to Kingero indicating that his thoughts were with his friends in Paris. It was that year that the 'Bulgarian Atrocities', to which he refers, occurred:

> I was in Paris during the elections for the Chamber, when a triumphant majority was returned, as of course you know, against that very bad, or very stupid person, Marshal Mac-Mahon. It was an interesting time you may imagine. On the morning of the elections, a manifesto of the President's came out. I was living at that time in what we call Bohemian style, buying and cooking my own food, and had occasion to go out early for some chocolate. When I read the proclamation, which was on the walls, I would have beaten MacMahon with my cane. It was a scandalous attempt to insult the poor people and so drive them to the barricades: if that was not the intention of the document, it was either written by a man out of his mind, or I do not know the meaning of words when I see them. They disappointed him for one while; but how is it all to end, who can foresee? I often have troubled moments over that; it touches me more immediately than the butcheries in Turkey; for I have very dear friends there, who may suffer inconvenience, or even hurt. [Letter to Kingero Fugicura 6th December, 1877]

Early the next year, 1878, RLS was in France with Fanny again. He reported in a letter that he was finishing *An Inland Voyage* in a hotel in Dieppe. In February he reported to his mother that he had been struggling for four days with the preface to it, and he was in correspondence with Colvin about a frontispiece for it. By May it was published. Indeed 1878 was a fecund year in which a number of his most significant early works were published.

In the summer of 1878 Stevenson acted as private secretary to Fleeming Jenkin, the Professor of Engineering at Edinburgh University, who was a member of one of the many International Juries at the Paris Exhibition, deciding which exhibits deserved medals. The World's Fair occupied more than twenty five hectares in the Champs de Mars where the Eiffel Tower now stands, and, north of the Seine, the Moorish Trocadero Palace, reincarnated as the Palais de Chaillot, was specially built for the Exhibition, and sold to Paris to defray expenses. On the Seine itself there was a variety of nautical exhibits. The Exhibition was on a far larger scale than any that had ever been held before. Unsurprisingly half of the exhibits were French; two thirds of the remainder came from Britain and the Colonies; and the Germans declined to participate. It was a resounding success, visited by

The Trocadero: erected for the Exhibition of 1878

thirteen million people, and it gloriously confirmed that France had recovered from the misfortunes of 1870-71.

The exhibition was due to open on 4th May, but it was not really ready until the beginning of June, when Jenkin and Stevenson seem to have arrived. 'The display of fine arts and machinery was upon a very large and comprehensive scale, and the Avenue des Nations, a street 2400 feet in length, was devoted to specimens of the architecture of nearly every country in Europe, and to several in Asia, Africa and America.' Quite what Stevenson did is not clear, but a close friend, fellow academic and fellow engineer, (Sir) Alfred Ewing commented wittily 'I had many letters from Jenkin in Paris, but none were written by the secretary.' Stevenson himself mentions going to the theatre with Fleeming Jenkin and 'when the piece was at an end, in front of a café in the mild midnight air, we had our fill of talk about the art of acting.' It was that year that Fanny, Belle and Lloyd, who spent their third summer beside the Loing, decided to return to the United States. This left Stevenson feeling very sorry for himself. He set off for the Cévennes, and was not to return to live in Paris.

In the summer of 1879 he passed through the city to stay, not in Fontainebleau, but at Cernay la Ville, near Rambouillet. Krøyer's portrait of him, one of the best, dates from this visit. Balfour confirms that, had he been able to find a companion he had thoughts of going to the Pyrenees,

51

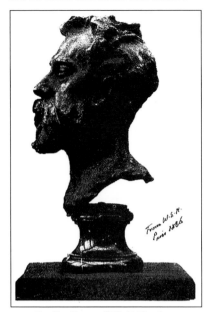

Rodin: Bust of W. E. Henley   **_Rodin: The Kiss_**

but this did not come to pass and, returning first of all to Britain, he abruptly departed for America where he eventually married Fanny Osbourne.

In 1881 he and his wife returned briefly to Paris via Fontainebleau, but went forthwith to St Germain-en-Laye where Fanny's little boy had been buried. They stayed in a hotel there, and RLS liked the place after Paris:

> A week in Paris reduced me to the limpness and lack of appetite peculiar to a kid glove, and gave Fanny a jumping sore throat...Well, the place (forest of beeches all new-fledged, grass like velvet fleets of hyacinth) pleased us and did us good.

Their last visit to the city in August 1886 was awkward because, owing to a piece of absent-mindedness on Stevenson's part, they were short of money, and rather embarrassingly dependent on the hospitality of Will Low and his wife in the Rue Vernier. Theodore Robinson, Low's fellow student at Carolus Duran's, was still in Paris – adopted as 'a quasi-permanent member' of the Low household – so there was talk of old times. However, there was recognition that they were times past; old fires not to be rekindled. Stevenson wrote a somewhat sombre poem about fires dedicated to Mrs Low, the only poem he ever wrote connected with Paris:

Even in the bluest noon day of July,
There could not run the smallest breath of wind
But all the quarter sounded like a wood;
And in the chequered silence and above
The hum of city cabs that sought the Bois,
Suburban ashes shivered into song.

Despite all this, the visit was not without some characteristic touches, or without a new contact, providing RLS with another link with the frontiers of fine art of his day. As Low relates, one reason for Stevenson's visit was to meet Henley whose own purposes included sitting for Auguste Rodin (1840-1917). The famous sculptor executed his most notorious sculpture, 'The Kiss' in the same year:

> It was through Henley that Stevenson, and incidentally Robinson and I, met Rodin. As the editor of the *Magazine of Art* Henley had endeavoured, as he expressed it, "to cram down the throats" of his subscribers some appreciation of the great French sculptor. It was a task foredoomed to failure, for the whole character of the respectable periodical whose fortunes he directed was essentially popular and middle class; and Henley had many tales of indignant protests from his scandalised readers, in whose views the publisher and the counting-house coincided so thoroughly that eventually the editorial advocacy of this and congenial forms of art brought about a rupture of their relations. The gallant campaign conducted by Henley had excited the gratitude of Rodin, however, and in return he had offered to model the bust of his protagonist; part of whose errand to Paris was to profit by this opportunity to secure so notable a portrait.

Low goes on to describe the sittings which took place:

> On different occasions Stevenson and I were present at the sittings for the bust, and as Rodin would pause in his work, his carefully considered and slowly uttered contribution to the more sprightly conversation of Henley and Stevenson gave me an impression that I had frequently experienced in talks with peasants... who are not prodigal of expression and prefer to wait until they are in full possession of the matter under consideration before they venture to reply.

In fact, Henley was more successful than Low supposed he might have been because, controversial as Rodin always remained, he got more support from the artistic community in Britain than from anywhere else, including France. 'Rodin undoubtedly met with his widest and most spontaneous response in England' [Bernard Champigneule 1967]. When the Royal Academy inadvertently refused to exhibit a Rodin sculpture that autumn, a correspondence ensued in *The Times*, in which one correspondent likened Rodin to Zola, which was regarded by Rodin's friends as a real insult. Stevenson let fly in a memorable way:

> His is no triumph of workmanship lending interest to what is base, but to an increasing degree as he proceeds in life, the noble expression of noble sentiment and thought. I was one of a party of artists that visited his studio the other day, and after having seen his later work, the "Dante", the "Paolo and Francesca", the "Printemps qui passe", we came forth again into the streets of Paris silenced, gratified, humbled in the thought of our own efforts, yet with a fine sense that the age was not utterly decadent, and that there were yet worthy possibilities in art. But, remark, it was not the sculptor we admired, nor was it of his skill, admirable and unusual as that is, that we talked as we went homeward. These questions of material talent had fallen below our thoughts, and the solemn face of the Dante over the great door still spoke to our imagination.
>
> The public are wary of statues that say nothing. Well here is a man coming forward whose statues live and speak things worth uttering. Give him time, spare him nicknames and the cant of cliques, and I venture to predict this man will take a place in the public heart.

Later during this visit to Paris Low and RLS entertained Rodin to lunch where, to Low's delight, Rodin expressed his admiration for their friend the sculptor, Gaudez. In the afternoon the party dawdled as far as the Pont des Arts where Low and Stevenson had first met. As RLS put it:

> Life is over, life was gay;
> We have come the primrose way.

He was never in Paris again, although even when he was in the South Seas he expressed the intention of returning there.

The Inland Voyage

Had the fun of the voyage
Had the sport of the boats
Who could have hoped in addition
The pleasure of Fing'ring the notes?

Stevenson always expressed himself as delighted and surprised that anyone should give him money for his early books. Indeed, the subject of his first book was the relatively unremarkable canoe trip which he and Sir Walter Simpson undertook on the rivers and canals of Belgium and northern France in 1876. It took place when RLS was already familiar with Paris, but, almost certainly, before he had met his future wife at Grès. It thus marks the end of his youth.

The trip may have been unremarkable, but RLS's account of it had the reviewers talking about Sterne. The district – a succession of growing industrial villages and towns – was undistinguished, and Stevenson was a young and ingenuous observer of 'foreign parts'. He was probably over-impressed, and inclined to moralise into the bargain. However, the succession of human incidents and wry observations contained in it were considered worth reading, and it has remained popular. Indeed it can be seen as one of the antecedents of *Three Men In A Boat*.

The French have always had a shrewd idea about which parts of their country appeal to Britons, and the A26, the 'Autoroute des Anglais', has recently been built in order to carry visitors, who know Provence much better than they know Picardy, southwards at great speed. The autoroute crosses RLS's route at Moy, where, in contrast, the two itinerants relaxed:

We lingered at Moy a good part of the day, for we were
fond of being philosophical, and scorned long journeys and
early starts on principle. The place, moreover, invited repose.
People in elaborate shooting costumes sallied from the château
with guns and game-bags; and this was a pleasure in itself,
to remain behind while these elegant pleasure seekers took
the first of the morning.

What were, in Stevenson's time, villages and small towns have all grown.
The district has been fought over twice, particularly during the 1914-18
war. It is changed and re-built; although there are several places where
the narrow Sambre-Oise canal – not the broader more modern ship canal
– can be found looking as it must have in his day. Although Stevenson
did not visit them, there are several places of considerable interest not
very far from the route. An attractive travel book by Andrew Sanger, including
the text of RLS's book, and called *An Inland Voyage* which describes this
sort of pilgrimage was published in 1991. It is delightfully illustrated, as
many of RLS's books have been. Here, the places in France visited by RLS
and his aristocratic companion are included in the gazetteer.

They entered France at Maubeuge where RLS was 'nearly taken up on
a charge of drawing the fortifications.' The two canoeists were accompanied
by the whole establishment of the hotel when they launched their canoes,
and they first followed the canalised Sambre to Quartes and Pont-sur-Sambre.
Nowadays the stretch between this village and Landrecies, passing through
the forest of Mormal, is amongst the least spoiled parts of the route. At
Landrecies they entered the Sambre and Oise canal. The weather was very
unkind to them: "when the rain was not heavy we counted the days almost
fair." It was thus not surprising that when they re-launched their canoes
at Vadencourt the Oise was in flood, and they came close to disaster.
They had a by-day at Origny, and continued their cruise to Moy, La Fère
and Noyon. Beyond Noyon the Oise becomes substantial, and by Compiègne,
RLS was complaining that they had forsaken the intimacy of the infant
river. However, the villages of Creil and Précy provided him with the intimacy
he craved. It is not surprising that what may have been intended to be
a trip, via the Seine, to Grèz was abandoned at Pontoise.

The 'Inland Voyage' became part of a great scheme which RLS had
in mind to cross France by its waterways and reach the Mediterranean.
It never came to fruition, but it was often in his mind.

Stevenson in France: Fontainebleau

It is highly characteristic of Stevenson that, in spite of the fact that he was an outsider, albeit one with a lively curiosity about art, he should have provided the Art World with a guide to one of its key sites – Fontainebleau in the late seventies and early eighties of the C19. He is still quoted as an authority long after most of the active participants, the painters themselves, have been forgotten. He saw himself, of course, as a legitimate art critic.

RLS described his experiences in Fontainebleau in letters, and in an early essay called *Forest Notes*. He reworked this material for a further article published in 1884, and used his experiences in a variety of ways in later work. There are also accounts of the same community in Will H. Low's book *A Chronicle of Friendships* [1908], and in others' recollections of Stevenson. R.A.M. Stevenson referred to the group in a more theoretical way in his criticisms of the way in which art students were trained in Britain in comparison with French students, and in an article about Grèz in the *Magazine of Art.*

Bob Stevenson's advocacy of the Impressionists in Britain referred to Fontainebleau. Although he wrote comparatively little about them, he was well aware, for example, that the painters who haunted Fontainebleau in the seventies and eighties were set in their ways, and that changes were being brought about elsewhere in France by painters like Manet.

> "...while men drowsed beneath the canopies of the forest in Barbizon or Marlotte, or wore Millet's spectacles on the plain of Chailly, already Manet had changed the face of painting."
> [R.A.M. Stevenson *Grèz* Magazine of Art 1893]

Bob met both Courbet and Millet, each of whom is considered to have influenced the Impressionists in different ways. These introductions were made possible by an American painter of the previous generation, William Babcock (1826-1899) who was friendly with Millet. Bob Stevenson's intellect was acknowledged by all who knew him. Fanny Stevenson, in a preface to *New Arabian Nights*, which originated partly in story-telling and talk at Grèz, and was dedicated 'to Robert Alan Mowbray Stevenson in grateful remembrance of their youth and their already old affection', wrote of him thus:

> It seems incredible that a genius so unusual as that of Robert Alan Mowbray Stevenson should pass out of existence, leaving nothing more for posterity than a single brilliant volume and a few desultory papers on music and painting; but he was a dreamer of dreams, without ambitions, who dwelt alone in a world of fantasy, from which he would sometimes emerge to dazzle his friends with wild theories, sound philosophy, unexpected learning, and whimsical absurdities, all jumbled together and presented with such pertinent reasoning and certainty of truth of his premises that his hearers would be swept off their feet.

It was in 1875 that Stevenson first went to Barbizon; later the same year he visited Grèz, and returned there in each of the three succeeding summers. At first, RLS seems to have been dependent upon Bob Stevenson, and overshadowed by him, but he found himself a role as an independent-minded literary commentator, and became a valued member of the group in his own right. However, when, for example, Bob went to Cernay la Ville in the spring of 1877, Louis went with him, rather than staying in Barbizon or Grèz. They were lively times, and it was a period in his life when he was basically well, and full of energy. They were years when he read a great deal, learned much about painting, and about France, and began to write productively.

RLS's original account, *Forest Notes*, written in Edinburgh, and published in *Cornhill* in May 1876, was personal. Will Low was disappointed with this piece, finding it rather ordinary. When Stevenson reworked some of this material for an article in the *Magazine of Art* in May/June 1884 it was tighter. It was retrospective, an article in which Stevenson described himself as 'an old-stager'. His views were professional in tone, but they are unlikely to have played a central role in the education of art students in Paris and Fontainebleau at the time, although they may have influenced some of them. That same summer, however, John Lavery exhibited 'On the Loing

– An Afternoon Chat', and Frank O'Meara's 'Evening in the Gâtinais' was shown at the Glasgow Institute of Fine Arts in 1884, and was widely discussed in artistic circles. The Forest of Fontainebleau was still a focal point for a significant number of artists. RLS puts Fontainebleau in perspective in his memorable way:

> One generation after another fall like honey-bees upon this memorable forest, rifle its sweets, pack themselves with vital memories, and when the theft is consummated depart again into life richer, but poorer also.

Stevenson's description begins with a reference to the period before the 'strange turn in the history of art' brought about by Impressionism, when Jean-François Millet (1814-1875) and Théodore Rousseau (1812-1867) were the leading artists established in Barbizon. Millet had died in the January of the year Stevenson first went to the forest and his loss was deeply felt amongst the artistic community. In *Forest Notes* Stevenson painted a word-picture of the theme of Millet's most famous works:

> The sun goes down, a swollen orange, as it were into the sea. A blue-clad peasant rides home, with a harrow smoking behind him among the dry clods. Another still works with his wife in their little strip. An immense shadow fills the plain; these people stand in it up to their shoulders; and their heads, as they stoop over their work and rise again, are relieved from time to time against the golden sky.

RLS goes on in his later essay to point out that Fontainebleau was probably chosen as a sketching ground because of its accessibility when the first railways were built, and expresses some surprise that, in spite of the fact that the railway network had by then extended to render incomparable landscapes elsewhere in France almost as accessible, Fontainebleau and Rambouillet remained the favoured districts. This he attributes, in part at least, to a quality, which the Forest of Fontainebleau still has, of being a wild place, but one not detached from civilisation.

Today Barbizon itself resembles Ambleside or Pitlochry, a holiday resort to which visitors flock, overtaxing the place. Yet, at the end of the Grande Rue the road – L'Allée des Vaches – still leads straight into the Forest, and it is not difficult to imagine Barbizon as it was when Stevenson, Low and others described it:

> Close to the edge of the forest, so close that the trees of the bornage stand pleasantly about the last houses, sits a certain

small and very quiet village. There is but one street, and that, not very long ago, was a green lane, where the cattle browsed between the doorsteps. As you go up this street, drawing ever nearer the beginning of the wood, you will arrive at last before the door of an inn where artists lodge.

In the Grande Rue, the Maison Ganne, the original artists' inn, stands semi-derelict awaiting conversion into a museum. A gnarled inn sign proclaims it to have been the resort, earlier than when RLS was there, of George Sand, the brothers Goncourt, Verlaine and Murger, the original bohemian and author of the stories on which *La Bohème* was based. It was as a result of the success of these stories that Murger was enabled to move to Marlotte where, like Stevenson after him, he became a literary man among artists. The great artists of the day, Corot, Rousseau, Millet, Charles Jacques and Rosa Bonheur, we are informed, also frequented the place.

Ganne's is, at present, a more convincing monument to its times than Siron's inn which, in Stevenson's day, was a humble 'artist's barrack' and is now an up-market international country hotel. Siron himself changed the name of the inn to L'Hôtel de l'Exposition in 1867 when local artists showed their work there. It became the Hôtellerie du Bas-Bréau in 1937, but the name, 'Stevenson's House', is still prominently displayed outside it. Quite what the artists who made the inn famous might have thought of that can be surmised. The Grande Rue consists of a mixture of elegant nineteenth century villas with private gardens, cottages and little shops.

Exposition Hotel: known to Stevenson as Siron's

1. BARBIZON — Hôtel de l'Exposition   E. L. D.

Every other building carries a commemorative plaque. The Hôtellerie du Bas-Bréau, in addition to being called Stevenson's House, carries a plaque recording that the Hungarian Ladislas de Paal (1846-1879) worked there 1873-77, reminding us what a cosmopolitan place Barbizon was. De Paal's friend, Mihaly Munkacsy (1844-1900) was probably the ablest painter working in Barbizon when Stevenson was there, although Gassies, a chronicler of the scene, was still active, but Courbet, Diaz de la Pena, and Jacque were old men.

Even the perspectives of the most accomplished critics are distorted with regard to their contemporaries. In connection with Barbizon Stevenson makes particular mention of Lachevre whose wife, Will Low points out, is the model for a character in *The Treasure of Franchard*, and his young contemporary Gaston Lafenestre (1841-1877), a landscape painter already dead, and buried alongside Rousseau and Millet. Another Barbizonian, Oliver de Penne (1831-1897), prone to drunken rages, is mentioned in connection with Marlotte.

RLS also included Cernay in his account of Fontainebleau, although it is some distance away, on the edge of the Forest of Rambouillet. The 'admirable' Pelouse – Léon Germain Pelouse (1838-1891) – is described by Stevenson as presiding over the colony of landscape artists there. He is now remembered by a fine statue 'erected by his friends and students' in the woods close to the tiny cascades near Cernay. The visitor can still find the Auberge de Paysagistes in the corner of the large square which, Stevenson considered, resembled the set for a comic opera. He did not care for Cernay very much, although he was there for some time twice.

The first students of Carolus-Duran, already identified, gathered at Barbizon in 1873 and 1874, and became known as 'the Anglo Saxons', a term intended to comprehend Americans and Canadians, Englishmen, Irishmen and Scotsmen. They were quartered at Siron's inn, where there were not only young French painters, but others from all over Europe and the Americas. Later additions to 'the Anglo-Saxons' included Henry Enfield, Middleton Jameson, and the younger Stevenson, Anthony Warton Henley, younger brother of W.E. Henley, and William Simpson, younger brother of Sir Walter Simpson, Bart., both of whom were Louis Stevenson's friends. Stevenson's account of Siron's dates from this period.

Low relates that it was the absence of water at Barbizon which led a party of them – the two Stevensons, Enfield, O'Meara, Walter Simpson, and Low – from Barbizon to the river at Grèz in August 1875, and Grèz became the place where they all went. It was at Grèz that Stevenson met his future wife the following summer. The group found, at the Hôtel Chevillon, as comfortable lodgings as at Siron's, and they made it their headquarters. Some indication of the quality of the inn, and the importance which was already attached to art was that, as Stevenson reported later, they found Guiseppe Palizzi (1812-1887), a lesser master, ensconced there in a studio which he had been permitted to build on the 'emplacement' for the 'jeu de boules'. Art was clearly held in high esteem at the Hôtel Chevillon.

It seems to have been during his first visit to Grèz that RLS went to Nemours, which he described in a letter to his mother:

> Nemours is a beautiful little town, watered by a great canal and a little river. The river is crossed by an infinity of little bridges, and the houses have courts and gardens, and come down in stairs to the very brim; and washerwomen sit everywhere in curious little penthouses and sheds. A sort of reminiscence of Amsterdam. The old castle turned now into a ballroom and cheap theatre; the seats of the pit (places are 1f and 2fs in this theatre) are covered with old Gobelins tapestry; one can still see the heads in the helmets. In the actors' dressing rooms are curious old Henry Fourth looking-glasses. On the other hand, the old manacles are now kept laid by in a box with a lot of flower-pots on top of it, in a room with four canary birds.

Hôtel Chevillon: the principal downstairs room

Hôtel Chevillon: the recently refurbished inn where RLS met Fanny Osbourne; now a study centre

The barge canal referred to links the Seine and the Loire across a low watershed, following the Loing almost to its source. This same route was followed by Walter Simpson, 'Cigarette', and Robert Louis Stevenson, 'Arethusa' in the summer of 1875 on a tramping holiday which foreshadowed the 'Inland Voyage' of the following year. It was doubtless at that time that the two made plans to cross France in two canoes because early the following year RLS was writing to Fanny Sitwell outlining their scheme:

> To the Highlands first, then to Antwerp; thence by canoe with Simpson, to Paris and Grèz (on the Loing, and an old acquaintance of mine on the skirts of Fontainebleau) to complete our cruise next spring if we're all alive and jolly by Loing and Loire, Saône and Rhône to the Mediterranean. It should make a jolly book of gossip.

The walking tour – via Chateau Renard, Châtillon-sur-Loing, and Gien to Châtillon-sur-Loire – was something of a fiasco, as Stevenson, who always had difficulties at frontiers and such like on account of his boyishness and his dishevelled appearance, was eventually arrested as a spy. He looked so like a beggar that he was charged just a 'halfpenny' for a drink by the landlady of one inn and felt he had stolen it; and his shady appearance led a postman to mistake him for a 'pornographic colporteur'. He was rescued from a dungeon in Châtillon-sur-Loire by the rather more convincing Simpson, but they were sent back to Paris on the train.

The story of the trip is contained, fittingly, in Epilogue to *An Inland Voyage*, although it took place earlier:

> The country where they journeyed, that green, breezy valley of the Loing, is one very attractive to cheerful and solitary people. The weather was superb; all night it thundered and lightened, and the rain fell in sheets; by day, the heavens were cloudless, the sun fervent, the air vigorous and pure.

Of the members of the 'Anglo Saxons' of Stevenson's day Frank O'Meara frequented Grèz longest. He and William Stott were key figures in the artistic community in Grèz when these young Scottish artists began to learn their craft there at the same time as Stevenson was pronouncing in the *Magazine of Art* that this was precisely what they might choose to do.

Nothing would have delighted Stevenson more than to have known that this was the case, and we have some evidence that he may have, for his article was illustrated by engravings by Anthony Warton Henley, including, of course, the old bridge, but also the delightful mill of Grèz, and a number of other forest scenes. Anthony Henley was another of Stevenson's acquaintances at Grèz. He had a modest talent, and we can suppose that his more successful older brother patronised him, as he also patronised Stevenson. On the other hand, Henley might well also have exercised his judgement in the matter, believing that he was on to something in identifying Grèz as a significant 'sketching ground' for British artists. It can also be noted that 'the Glasgow Boys' gravitated later to Cambuskenneth on the Forth with its old abbey, its orchards and a picturesque ferry which might, by a man on a galloping horse at least, have been described as a Scottish 'Grèz'. Edward Walton and Arthur Melville had studios there. This, too, for sentimental reasons, would have pleased Stevenson who spent a good deal of time in his boyhood near Stirling.

This charming French village was central to the development of some of the Glasgow Boys at the same time as Stevenson was painting word pictures of the place in the *Magazine of Art*, and elsewhere.

Lavery's mention of Harrison, of Hawkins and of Larsson is significant in connection with Stevenson. Birge Harrison wrote an article about his experiences in Grèz, recalling Stevenson. He definitely met Stevenson in April 1881 when RLS and Fanny paid a sentimental return visit to Siron's, and he gives an account of the period when the two Stevensons were at Chevillon's together. Fernande Sadler states that Alexander Harrison, his older brother who achieved some notoriety by using nude models in the open air, stayed in Grèz 1881-1884, but, although she mentions Birge Harrison, she does not say exactly when he was in Grèz.

Larsson and Hawkins stuck in Harrison's mind, as they had stuck in Lavery's, although Larsson was definitely not in Grèz when Stevenson was. However, he was the most important of a group of Swedish artists who, like 'the Anglo-Saxons' found the village to their liking, and seem to have succeeded 'the Anglo Saxons' in dominating the place. Interestingly enough they also possessed, in August Strindberg (1849-1912), a prominent writer who became an intimate member of the colony. Carl Larsson (1853-1919) arrived in Grèz in April, 1882, and, like Palizzi, he secured a permanent studio there which was built on to the pension, with a balcony overlooking the river. It was Strindberg's early friendship for Larsson that brought him to Grèz, and it is the Swedish connection with Chevillon's – Larsson's in particular – which has led to the present restoration which has been undertaken by the 'Fondation Grèz sur Loing' of Gothenburg in Sweden.

Harrison goes on to make particular mention of two other Swedish painters, both women, Emma Løwstädt (1855-1931), and a Mlle Lillenthal whom he connects with Fanny Osbourne: all three were pioneers – members of their sex who were painters rather than models or hangers-on. Emma Løwstädt secured the studio which was built in the garden of Chevillon's for Joseph Palizzi. She married another American, Francis Brook Chadwick (b.1850) and resided in Grèz for many years. This couple may both appear in a famous photograph showing Chevalier Palizzi, Bob Stevenson and Frank O'Meara by the river at the foot of the garden of the inn.

Stevenson's own accounts of Grèz make no mention either of Salis or of Robinson. However, such stories as narrated by both Low and Harrison illuminate those years in a particular way, and put Stevenson's experiences in a lively artistic context. R.A.M. Stevenson, in his article about Grèz, dwells on the place, as a critic, in a rather more abstract and theoretical fashion, pronouncing about its place in art history:

> Grèz was a half-way between the forest and the Seine. Lodged on a tributary with less formal banks than the big river, it showed a greater variety of view in a small length, slenderer and more elegant tree-forms, but narrower horizons and less evident construction in the distance. Corot seemed to be the genius of the place. His spirit of grace hung about the slim supple stems, the bowery foliage, the shaded pools, the long grasses, the waving reeds, and all the cloudy vaporous growths of river-banks, swamps and fields.

He goes on to describe the way in which, whereas Barbizon, Marlotte and Cernay remained essentially French, Grèz was taken over by Anglo-Saxons and to point out that undoubtedly the place and the ideals fostered there had, as we have seen, considerably influenced British art. There is, however, a great deal of warmth in his description of Palizzi which elaborates RLS's brief reference to the same master in Fontainebleau:

> When I first knew Grèz, the Chevalier G. Palizzi, one of the old men of 1830, lived in a pavilion on the terrace of the ancient inn garden. He was the patriarch of the place and much visited by men of letters and painters. Himself no mean painter, and a man of age and distinction, he was yet the most genial comrade you could wish. Entirely free, like most French painters, from stiffness and any affectation of superiority, he placed his wit, his knowledge of life, and his advice on art at the service of the youngest and most obscure beginners. Robust in figure, with wide-tossed white hair, he reminded me of Corot with whom he had been much associated in the past. [R.A.M. Stevenson *Grèz* 1893]

The Forest of Fontainebleau owes its character to an outcrop of sandstones which geologically resemble in some respects the North Downs around

Moret sur Loing: laveuses at work beside the river

27. MORET-sur-LOING — Le Pont et les Laveuses

Tunbridge Wells. Indeed, there are similar heaths and forests there, and similar fantastically shaped rocks. At the foot of the North Downs is a clay plain. Its equivalent in France is a clay plain once dotted with ponds or meres called 'gatines', hence the pays is called the Gâtinais. It is drained by a minor tributary of the Seine called the Loing. Grèz is situated on the very edge of the Gâtinais, built of dull grey sandstone on which the sun does, however, shine in the summer, giving the place a great deal of charm. Nemours and Moret, and even Montigny, all situated on the Loing as well, have grown and changed a good deal since Stevenson's day. Bourron and Marlotte are very suburban, and Barbizon a tourist trap. Grèz has succeeded in retaining its character, and much of Stevenson's description [in *Forest Notes*] holds good today:

> And Grèz when we get there, is indeed a place worthy of some praise. It lies out of the forest, a cluster of houses with an old bridge, an old castle in ruin, and a quaint old church. The inn garden descends in terraces to the river; stable-yard, kailyard, orchard, and a space of lawn, fringed with rushes and embellished with a green arbour. On the opposite bank there is a reach of English-looking plain, set thickly with willows and poplars. And between the two lies the river, clear and deep, and full of reeds and floating lilies. Water-plants cluster about the sterlings of the long low bridge, and stand half-way up on the piers in green luxuriance.

In every way Grèz seems to have been an ideal place in which to spend the long summer days of one's youth. Bob Stevenson, a Cambridge man, notes that the Loing reminded him of the Cam, although it is deeper than that river. For that reason rowing boats, dinghies or skiffs – chaloupes (shallops) – and canoes, rather than punts, were used, and the 'Anglo-Saxons' soon devised races similar to those held at the older universities. Swimming, or rather splashing about, was another outdoor recreation, as were a variety of competitive garden games including leap frog and other muscular activities. Indoors the centrepiece of the ground floor of the Hôtel Chevillon – it was rebuilt during Bob Stevenson's lifetime – was the Billiards Room, which acted as a wet-weather studio, and as the setting for charades and dramatic performances. Off it were smaller rooms, a dining room on one side and a bar on the other. Painting and drawing activities were interspersed with active debate and wild recreation, or, according to some accounts, artistic activities took place in intervals between these highly enjoyable ways of spending one's time. A further dimension to the place was provided by what may be considered its Bohemianism: the wearing of outrageous clothes, the flouting of convention and the pursuit of the opposite sex. In his biography of John Singer Sargent, Richard Ormond suggests that Sargent 'was almost certainly one of the group from Carolus-Duran's atelier who went to Barbizon in the early summer of 1875'. Sargent wrote a letter of 16 August 1881 to Vernon Lee [Violet Paget] about Grèz:

> It is very pretty, but a nest of bohemians, English bohemians, who will sweep down upon you. Tel le vautour [Like the vulture]. You will meet the irresistible O'Meara and my very good friend Arthur Heseltine. You will probably be introduced to these gentlemen's heads bobbing about with hats on, for they are all the time bathing from your garden. There are two inns at Grèz the disreputable and the semi-reputable, the former is called Chez Chevillon, the latter Chez Laurent. And now heaven protect you.

"There was," reported Birge Harrison, "a certain return to primitive standards in the relation between the sexes." Bob Stevenson puts the matter thus:

> Many writers could tell you that they found those colonies as fitted for the study of the human heart as of trees and rocks. You saw the very bones and muscles of the passions laid bare. But such anatomy disgusts the true Englishman. He dislikes this want of reserve...

In such a context Robert Louis Stevenson's love affair with Fanny Osbourne was probably more ordinary than it has subsequently been made out to be. It is at once one of the most oft told of literary romances, and one of the least known about. The eye-witnesses appear to agree about some things, but on examination it is almost certain that what they seem to agree about was probably not true. Later speculation has tended to cloud the issue rather than to clarify it.

Stevenson himself, added various unique qualities to the situation. Birge Harrison writing much later, and, as has already been suggested, confusing things a little, was quite clear that he did not then suppose that Louis would become a famous man, and it is possible to infer that neither he nor Will Low, nor others who were present, supposed that the less impressive of the two cousins would become Fanny Osbourne's lover. Of course, looking back at the affair we know how it came out. Stevenson ended up in the South Seas with the woman concerned (who was ten years older than him), her daughter (who was seven years younger than him, and to whom he was at one time attracted), and his mother (a parent disapproving of the involvement in the first place). They all outlived him. The emotional possibilities of a love-affair which was going to end like this are immense. Such relationships no doubt occur often enough, but Stevenson has offered his friends and the public some account of his feelings which has given the affair a public quality which has rendered it unusual. Early on, for example, we find Fanny writing to a friend, noting that RLS had written a magazine article about her daughter.

He publicised his feelings about himself as if he felt compelled to do so, without, however, really illuminating the relationship at Grèz very much. This was in part because he disguised what was happening from others at the time. Furthermore his passions were such – he was still emotionally involved with Fanny Sitwell when he met Fanny Osbourne – that it is not possible to be quite sure whether all were genuine, or none. What can safely be said is that Stevenson met Fanny Osbourne at Grèz, and became very close to her and, perforce, to her family. Three years later he went half way across the world and married her. Whatever emotional drive brought these events about, he displayed at the same time an equally powerful determination to become a writer.

It was during the summer of 1875, although that was also the year when the group spent much more time in Barbizon than in Grèz, that the 'Anglo Saxons' seem to have identified the Pension Chevillon as their own, and to have become sufficiently familiar with the geography to feel that they owned the place, in the way that groups of students do. By the following summer Will Low was describing the scene as follows:

> Meanwhile in Grèz the Anglo Saxon was in full possession of Chevillon's inn, to a much greater degree than Barbizon ever knew. Not only the men who first 'discovered' Grèz, but others, brought to the quiet inn the clamour of our English tongue, and a freedom of manners and customs that escapes geographical definition. This independence of conduct, to the astonishment of the rural population, they maintained at all times; ignoring completely the usages which, rude and simple as they are, centuries have imposed on the orderly country...Behind the inn, in the long garden stretching to the river, the table was spread and here a score or more would be seated for the midday meal, in the lightest of costumes, fresh from a dip in the river. [W.H. Low *A Chronicle of Friendships* 1908]

In her biography of her sister, Fanny Stevenson (1840-1914), Nellie V. de G. Sanchez states that Grèz was recommended to her by an American sculptor called Pardessus on the grounds that it was not only inexpensive, but quiet and out-of-the-way, and that when she went there in May 1876, accompanied by her daughter Belle, aged seventeen, and her son Lloyd, aged eight, she found just one other painter, Walter Palmer (1854-1932), a refugee from Duran's atelier, at work. Sam Osbourne, Fanny's first husband, seems to have been there early on, and then to have returned to the United States.

None of this fits in very well with the picture of Fanny and Belle arriving as intruders among a colony of painters. Various rather unlikely accounts have Bob Stevenson hearing about their arrival, and going to Grèz with the intention of freezing out the newcomers if he did not find them sufficiently agreeable, on the grounds that they were members of the opposite sex. He encountered Belle first, and the two women seem to have won his approval easily enough. Low reports that he and his wife joined Bob one evening at Chevillon's, and found the women ensconced at the other end of the dining table, with Bob apologetically explaining to Low that they were 'of the right sort'. It was Low who is said to have conveyed this information to RLS in Paris in July of the same year before he, too, hurried to Grèz, and met his future wife for the first time. He said later that he glimpsed her through the window and was taken with her from the first; and perhaps he did:

> One evening in the summer of 1876 the little party of guests at the old inn sat at dinner about the long table in the centre of the salle à manger with the painted panels – the handiwork of artists who had stopped there at various times. It was a soft sweet evening and the doors and windows were open; dusk drew near and the lamps had just been lit. Suddenly a young man approached from outside. It was Robert Louis Stevenson, who afterwards admitted that he had fallen in love with his wife at first sight when he saw her in the lamplight through the open window. [Nellie Sanchez *Life of Mrs R.L. Stevenson* 1920]

However, other accounts have this incident taking place at the conclusion of Simpson and Stevenson's 'Inland Voyage' in the autumn of 1876. Relationships between the principals seem to have been complicated at first, as is often so. The highly attractive Belle was taken with both of the Stevensons, and she became infatuated with Frank O'Meara. Fanny wrote much more about the handsome Bob in her early letters to the United States, while Bob Stevenson seems to have fallen in love with Belle. Indeed relationships may well have been even more complicated than that because subsequent accounts have all come from sources closely connected with Stevenson, rather than from the histories of other artists.

Will Low, who was an acute enough observer of what was going on, comments that he saw little of Fanny or of Belle that summer, although he was a visitor himself, not staying at the inn. Belle wrote about either RLS or Bob Stevenson in a letter to the United States:

> There is a young Scotchman here, a Mr Stevenson, who looks at me as though I were a natural curiosity. He never saw a real American girl before, and he says I act and talk as though I came out of a book – I mean an American book. He says that when he first met Bloomer he came up to him and said in his western way: 'These parts don't seem much settled, hey?' He laughed for an hour at the idea of such an old place not being much settled. He is such a nice looking ugly man, and I would rather listen to him talk than read the most interesting book I ever saw. We sit in the little green arbor after dinner drinking coffee and talking till late at night. [Nellie Sanchez]

In addition to probably talking to her late into the night, RLS took Belle for a trip to Nemours in his 'Rob Roy' canoe as well. Belle, much later in life, and probably re-writing history on the way things were at Grèz introduces *Travels with a Donkey*, although Fanny may have made this remark later:

> It is romantic rubbish that Louis fell in love with my mother when he glimpsed her through a window, though she may have made an attractive picture in the lamplight. She was simply a foreigner from a country he had never seen... And my mother, her life marred by infidelity, was immune to any amorous regard. Fact is, as their acquaintance progressed, she considered his stories of his travels with his donkey naïve as compared with her own adventures. And when he interrupted her sketching with questions about America and the Indians he was a nuisance.

Belle goes on to describe how Lloyd was spoiled by the attentions of the men, which often caused both of them to be confined to their quarters. She also states that she was only allowed to swim in her discreet bathing dress when the family were quite alone, as they were most of the time.

Fanny was recovering from the shock resulting from the death in Paris of her younger son. She seems to have been a centre of polite attention at Chevillon's. Again, Belle described the scene in a contemporaneous letter:

We generally congregate down in the garden by the big tree after dinner. Mama swings in the hammock, looking as pretty as possible, and we all form a group around her on the grass, Louis and Bob babbling about boats, while Simpson, seated near by, fans himself with a large white fan.

Later that summer Fanny began to refer more frequently in letters to Bob Stevenson. In October she and Bob got lost on a walk in the Forest which she later reported, in a letter to the States, she had not embarked upon for purposes of flirtation. Clearly there were others who believed that she had. RLS and Walter Simpson had undertaken the canal trip which formed the basis for the book *An Inland Voyage* in September, and returned to Grèz. Bob – for self-protection, perhaps – impressed on Fanny the virtues of his younger cousin. He may have had reason to suppose, from indications he had received from either of them, or from both of them, that there was the basis for a relationship there. However, at that time, Louis is reported to have been liable to burst into tears, or to have uncontrollable fits of hysterical laughter. For her part Fanny does seem to have applied herself to art, the most substantial result being a picture of the Bridge at Grèz executed in 1876/7 which is in the Stevenson museum in Edinburgh. She also made a sketch of Louis that summer which was later re-drawn by

Cernay-la-Ville

Theodore Blake Wirgman (1848-1925), an artist of Swedish origin who worked as an illustrator for the *Graphic*, and who, by co-incidence, also frequented Grèz. In it he is wearing his Indian smoking cap and his velvet jacket and cuts a strange figure. He impressed his friends in many ways, but he does seem to have been odd and less impressive, in any case, than Bob. It is difficult to believe that Louis and Fanny could be described as having fallen in love that summer.

In the autumn of '76 the painters returned to Paris, Fanny taking her children to live in an apartment in Montmartre. This was when Low first referred to his impossible passion and when he returned to Edinburgh RLS wrote *On Falling In Love*; he was probably, from then on, very much in love with Fanny Osbourne. However, it is clear from her letters that, unless she was disguising her feelings very well, Fanny's regard for Louis may not have been as great. In the spring of the following year she was still mentioning both cousins in letters, while each of them was commending the other, but it has been suggested that, by that time, she and Louis must have been lovers. Belle, quoted in later life, painted a rather different picture.

At Grèz a major topic of conversation the previous autumn had been the possibility of purchasing a barge to act as a sort of floating artists' colony. The idea originated with Bob Stevenson after the return of Louis Stevenson and Walter Simpson from their trip, and was taken up enthusiastically. The shareholders in this enterprise became Henry Enfield, Sir Walter Simpson and the two Stevensons, and the barge was purchased, probably in Nemours, the next year, in the summer of 1877. That year Stevenson spent February, then June and July in France. Early on Bob and Louis went to Cernay-la-Ville, whence Bob went to Barbizon, and thence to Grèz. Low was less enthusiastic about Grèz that summer which had been invaded by a new crowd. Louis returned to Paris, then the Osbournes went, for the second summer, to Grèz.

Simpson was landed with putting up most of the money for the barge, and it was he and Louis who supervised the work on their 'day-dream'. It was named *The Eleven Thousand Virgins of Cologne*. RLS was in Cologne as a boy, but it is more likely that he and Simpson learned of the unlikely legend of St. Ursula, the English Princess, who was allegedly martyred with eleven thousand of her fellow countrywomen (more likely she, and another woman) in Cologne. The barge was taken to Moret, further downstream on the Loing, for refurbishment, 'under the walls of the ancient town', where the two of them, presumably based at Grèz, idled away their time. Low was pressed into service to decorate the panels of one of the cabins which was to be known as 'the bridal chamber'.

Moret became in 1889 the home of Alfred Sisley (1839-1899), the Impressionist painter who, in the late seventies, was painting at Veneux nearby. Sisley captured the special atmosphere of the Loing at Moret where it is still possible to linger beside the old bridge with its weirs and mills, an impressive town-gate, and the nineteenth century washing-place and envisage the young entrepreneurs dreaming about their floating home. RLS wrote later to Simpson:

> "...and you will not have forgotten the amount of sweet champagne consumed in the inn at the bridge end to give zeal to the workmen and speed to the work." [*Inland Voyage*]

The project foundered because of lack of capital, and the carpenter of Moret was said to have seized the vessel, and, more sadly, the two canoes, in which Simpson and Stevenson had made their epic journey, and sold them to pay his bills. It is surmised by biographers that it was during this summer that Louis and Fanny floated down the Loing in a canoe, and sealed their relationship. One of Stevenson's *New Poems*, published after his death contains the lines:

> Mine eyes were swift to know thee, and my heart
> As swift to love. I did become at once
> Thine wholly, thine unalterably, thine
> In honourable service, pure intent,
> Steadfast excess of love and laughing care:
> And as I was, so am, and so shall be.
> I knew thee helpful, knew thee true, knew thee
> And Pity bedfellows: I heard thy talk
> With answerable throbbings. On the stream
> Deep, swift and clear, the lilies floated; fish
> Through the shadows ran. There, thou and I
> Read Kindness in our eyes and closed the match.

In the early autumn Fanny returned to Paris and Louis followed her. Thus throughout that year the relationship between the two must have developed. It was in October that Fanny took Louis into her Montmartre apartment to nurse an eye infection. Then his illness meant that they had to return to England. Early the next year, 1878, RLS was in France again, and he had the opportunity to return to France in the summer as the secretary to his friend Professor Fleeming Jenkin in Paris. Afterwards he went to Grèz. However, Fanny, whose father had died, and whose husband had stopped sending her money, was forced to return to the United States in

July. Stevenson's parents were no doubt delighted for they did not at that time approve of his relationship with her; Louis was devastated. He went that autumn to the Cévennes and expressed some of his devastation in asides in *Travels with a Donkey*. In later years Fanny and Louis must have often spoken about Grèz. They paid a further fleeting visit together to the Forest of Fontainebleau in April, 1881 when they encountered Harrison at Siron's. They never visited Grèz again, but they will always be strongly associated with the place.

Will Low summed up this period of Robert Louis Stevenson's life neatly:

> He made fitful appearances in Paris, and in the intervals came
> the Inland Voyage, the meeting with his future wife, the stories
> strongly tinctured by the land where we dwelt, and his essays
> picturing the life we led... [W.H. Low quoted in R. Masson
> *I Can Remember Robert Louis Stevenson* 1925]

Earlier in 1877 Stevenson contributed a series of minor articles to a magazine called *London* in which some of his most important early work was published. These included *A Ball at Mr Elsinare's*, the article describing Belle Osbourne. In 1878 he traversed the area again on his way to the Cévennes. *The Song of the Road*, with its references to the quintessentially Scottish gauger [exciseman], might be a song of travel set in his native land, but this, the second poem in *Underwoods*, his first collection of verse, was composed in the Forest of Montargis.

Underwoods was collected at a later date, but Stevenson told Low that he was thinking of the American's house at Montigny when he wrote the charming *Envoy*:

> Go, little book, and wish to all
> Flowers in the garden, meat in the hall,
> A bin of wine, a spice of wit,
> A house with lawns enclosing it,
> A living river by the door,
> A nightingale in the sycamore!

Surely *The Canoe Speaks* contains echoes of the Loing, as well. Stevenson might be, although he cannot be, describing Alexander Harrison's models posing out of doors, or William Stott's 'Bathers':

> By willow wood and water-wheel
> Speedily fleets my touching keel;
> By all retired and shady spots

> Where prosper dim forget-me-nots;
> By meadows where at afternoon
> The growing maidens troop in June
> To loose their girdles on the grass
> Ah! speedier than before the glass
> The backward toilet goes, and swift
> As swallows quiver, robe and shift
> And the rough country stockings lie
> Around each young divinity.

Three lines excised from the poem after 'on the grass', and said to render it more sexy than it was, run as follows:

> And stepping free each breathing lass
> From her discarded ring of clothes
> Into the crystal coolness goes

The poem is probably more interesting as it stands, apart from the obvious difficulty posed by three lines rather than two couplets. He sent it to Low in April, 1884, expressing the hope that he would illustrate it, and saying: "Some riverside will haunt you and O! be tender to my bathing girls."

Both Harrison and Low tell us that it was at Chevillon's that the *New Arabian Nights* were conceived, although Stevenson himself mentioned conversations in Chelsea with Bob. This was his first extended piece of fiction and his first venture into the fantastic, the extravagant and the rather macabre. The story of the 'Suicide Club' originated, it is said, in the fertile brain of Bob Stevenson, and Robert Louis Stevenson noted down this, and other tales during summer evenings at Grèz. In 1909 the story was made into a Grand-Guignol play *Les Nuits du Hampton Club* by two French playwrights Mouezy-Eon and Armont. At about the same time he wrote two other short stories *Will o' the Mill* and *The Sire de Maltroit's Door*, the latter being published in book form with the *New Arabian Nights*. It was originally called *The Sire de Maltroit's Mousetrap* and is a romantic comedy set in fifteenth century France. Characteristically he put the finishing touches to the story at a distance, on holiday in Cornwall.

If these pieces all owe something to Fontainebleau, there are others which owe more to it. In *New Poems* we find that RLS essayed a 'word-picture' of the object of so many of his artist friends' paintings – 'The Bridge at Grèz'. It is not surprising that he suppressed it, as it is not a very good poem – not quite in the same class as MacGonagall's river poems, although it is reminiscent of them, and the whole thing is rather like a cheerful hymn about a solemn subject – and, in spite of that, very interesting in this context:

> Know you the river near to Grèz,
>   A river deep and clear?
> Among the lilies all the way,
> That ancient river runs today
>   From snowy weir to weir.
>
> Old as the Rhine of great renown,
>   She hurries clear and fast,
> She runs amain by field and town,
> From south to north, from up to down.
>   To present on from past
>
> The love I hold was borne by her;
>   And now, though far away,
> My lonely spirit hears the stir
> Of water round the starling spur
>   Beside the Bridge at Grèz.
>
> So may that love forever hold
>   In life an equal pace;
> So may that love grow never old,
> But clear and pure and fountain-cold,
>   Go on from grace to grace.

Forest Notes was, of course, the product of Barbizon and Grèz, so too was *Village Communities of Painters: Fontainebleau* in which he developed the first piece into a more considered description of the artists' colonies of the district. It is interesting that Leslie Stephen, the mountaineer and editor of *Cornhill*, infuriated the young Stevenson by pointing out that he only liked parts of *Forest Notes*, and that he proposed to cut it. How right the older man was, for *Forest Notes* remains rather a boring read. Stevenson clearly learned the lesson because *Fontainebleau* is sharper. It can also be pointed out that Henley arranged for *Fontainebleau* to be copiously illustrated, and, in its original form in the *Magazine of Art*, it has much more impact, as would several of Stevenson's earlier pieces, than in the dull collections of prose in which it normally appears.

Another rather opaque early poem written in 1875-76 has been connected with *Forest Notes*, although it might, as easily, recall the tramp through the Gâtinais of the same period:

> In autumn when the woods are red
> And the skies are grey and clear,
> The sportsmen seek the wild fowls' bed
> Or follow down the deer;
> And cupid hunts by haugh and head,
> By riverside and mere,
> I walk, not seeing where I tread
> And keep my heart with fear,
> Sir, have an eye on where you tread,
> And keep your heart with fear,
> For something lingers here;
> A touch of April not yet dead,
> In autumn when the woods are red
> And skies are grey and clear.

Providence and the Guitar is a story which Stevenson based on the history of a pair of strolling players called De Vauversin who visited Chevillon's. Stevenson felt sorry for the impoverished actors described in the tale, and, with characteristic generosity, he sent the proceeds from the story, written and published in 1878, to them.

The Treasure of Franchard is set in the Forest of Fontainebleau. It contains a really effective picture of French provincial life, displaying the understanding of and love for France which Stevenson had. He is said to have based the irregular, 'common-law', marriage in the story on that of the Lachèvres. It was, however, quite usual for the consent of the parents to be withheld, and for couples to live together until their parents died when they then got married; it applied to Millet as well. The story contains an affectionate description of Grèz:

> The river, as blue as heaven, shone here and there among the foliage. The indefatigable birds turned and flickered about Gretz church-tower. A healthy wind blew from over the forest, and the sound of innumerable thousands of tree-tops and innumerable millions on millions of green leaves was abroad in the air, and filled the ear with something between whispered speech and singing. It seemed as if every blade of grass must hide a cigale; and the fields rang merrily with their music, jingling far and near with as with the sleigh-bells of the fairy

queen. From their station on the slope the eye embraced a large space of poplar'd plain upon the one hand, the waving hill-tops of the forest on the other, and Gretz itself in the middle, a handful of roofs. [*The Treasure of Franchard* 1883]

He did not write *The Treasure of Franchard* until he was in Kingussie in 1882 on the last occasion he was in the Highlands of Scotland, finishing it in France, when he and Fanny were in Marseilles. This is typical enough, indeed Stevenson very rarely wrote about places where he was at the time. Of course, he included a reference to Fontainebleau in *The Wrecker*, the novel he and Lloyd wrote in the South Seas, the early scenes of which are set in the Paris he knew. The railway put Fontainebleau in close touch with Paris, and the young art students in the story set off, late one hot summer afternoon, for Fontainebleau on the spur of the moment:

> ...the remainder of the company crowded the benches of a cab; the horse was urged, as horses have to be, by an appeal to the pocket of the driver; the train caught by the inside of a minute; and in less than an hour and a half we were breathing deep of the sweet air of the forest, and stretching our legs up the hill from Fontainebleau octroi [toll-house], bound for Barbizon. [Lloyd Osbourne and R.L. Stevenson *The Wrecker* 1892]

Stevenson's acute recall is part of his artistry, though he and Fanny can never have had any difficulty in recalling Grèz, and he wistfully recalled Grèz both in the poem dedicated to Will Low and in the similar fragment dedicated to his wife of 1889:

> Long must elapse ere you behold again
> Green forest frame the entry of the lane-
> The wild lane with the bramble and the briar,
> The year-old cart-tracks perfect in the mire,
> The wayside smoke, perchance, the dwarfish huts,
> And ramblers' donkey drinking from the ruts:
> Long ere you trace how deviously it leads,
> Back from man's chimneys and the bleating meads
> To the woodland shadow, to the sylvan hush,
> When but the brooklet chuckles in the brush-
> Back from the sun and bustle of the vale
> To where the great voice of the nightingale
> Fills all the forest like a single room,

And all the banks smell of the golden broom;
So wander on until the eve descends,
And back returning to your firelit friends,
You see the rosy sun, despoiled of light,
Hung, caught in thickets, like a schoolboy's kite.

[To My Wife: A Fragment 1889]

As he put it in his epilogue, dedicated to Low, in *The Wrecker* Stevenson was always 'a little pleased to breathe once more the airs of our youth.'

Note on the orthography of the name 'Grèz': The spelling currently adopted by the IGN is 'Grèz-sur-Loing', but the spelling 'Grès' was, at one time, frequently used. The anglicisation 'Gretz' was current in Stevenson's day, and is occasionally retained in quotations.

Stevenson in the Cévennes

> On the whole this is a Scottish landscape, although not so
> noble as the best in Scotland [*A Mountain Town in France*]

Stevenson is still a presence in the Cévennes. He can be sought out by
those who chose to do so in a way that only Scott and Burns – not
Wordsworth, let alone Jules Verne – can be found in Scotland. Indeed,
Stevenson himself is better celebrated in the Cévennes than he is in the
Highlands of Scotland. This is not a matter of celebrating famous sons –
Gévaudan is Marcel Pagnol country, for example – but of acknowledging
associations. *Travels with a Donkey*, which, although a slim volume, was
one of his first proper books, is for many readers their first introduction
to Stevenson, remembered with affection.

Although the reader is reminded that it is about France, it is a universal
sort of book which might be about many places. RLS does not really address
what he calls elsewhere the 'spread landscape', and many of his readers
may not be clear about where the Cévennes are, or even, what they are.
Perhaps he is leaving such questions for the reader to address later, as
many of them have.

Several writers, including Richard Holmes, who followed Stevenson's
itinerary closely, point out that part of the Cévennes which Stevenson
traversed is rather ordinary in comparison with other parts of the district,
but this fits in with his philosophy, and the famous Scottish author has,
of course, created his own associations with it.

Stevenson would probably be well-pleased with the treatment he gets
in Le Monastier, where he spent about a month before setting out on his

Le Monastier

Travels With a Donkey. Here is none of the brash technology of some modern Visitor Centre, where interpretation tends to obscure rather than enlighten. He gets a room devoted to him in a genuine country museum and there is a memorial, as a result of the efforts of the Stevenson Society of Edinburgh, in the Mairie. These are a consequence of the elaborate centenary celebrations of 1978 the effect of which Richard Holmes deplored:

> The well-meaning attempt to conserve or recover the past can be more subtly destructive. Since the centenary of Stevenson's *Travels* I am told the whole route has been marked out, by the local Syndicats d'Initiative, with a series of blazed stakes which lead the pilgrim from one picturesque point de vue to the next, and bring him safely down each evening to some recommended hotel, Carte Touristique, hot bath, and Souvenirs Cévenols. I have not had the heart to go back and see.

Some years on this does not seem to be quite fair. Holmes was of course writing as a biographer of the difficulties of getting to grips with the realities of a personality, and there are echoes of what he says, too, in the arguments which the 'hill men' always put up in Scotland when some new interpretative venture is proposed for their beloved Highlands. That the French method of waymarking is very crude can be granted, but this is the way in which they mark all of their paths. Twelve years after it was established the Stevenson Trail is simply one of several French interconnected long distance paths.

Holmes goes on to observe that times change:

> This physical presence is none the less extremely deceptive. The material surfaces of life are continually breaking down, sloughing off, changing, almost as fast as human skin. A building is restored, a bridge rebuilt or replaced, a road is widened or re-routed, a forest is cut down, a wooded hill is built over, a village green becomes a town centre. Stevenson's La Trappe had been burnt down, redesigned and rebuilt; many of his donkey tracks had become tarred roads; his wild upland heaths had been planted over; and even his terraces of deep chestnut trees had been replaced by the commercial foresting of young pines.

However, Stevenson would surely have been delighted that the twentieth century pilgrim should be required to exercise her or his imagination in order to properly grasp the associations of the place with the young écrivain écossais and Modestine a hundred years previously. Things do change, and Stevenson was not travelling in the age of the motor car and the video recorder, but we sometimes need to remind ourselves that he was travelling in the age of the telegraph and the railway train. By the centenary of his death in 1994 the Motorway will have reached the Cévennes. Further north, near Brioude, a motorway viaduct has been built striding across one of the headwaters of the Dordogne as, in Stevenson's time, railway navvies were throwing bridges across the rivers of the Cévennes along the very route that he took. He would not be surprised if we boarded the Cévenol Express during our journey, as the Syndicat d'Intiative recommend.

The Cévennes is a series of mountain ranges which form the south-eastern part of the Massif Central. Like many old land names it is a vague term which has been somewhat abused. It certainly comprehends much of the modern Departments of Haute Loire, Lozère and Gard, but such names, like our own more recent regional and district names, are still lacking in atmosphere or proper association. It suffers, as, say, the Grampians or the Trossachs suffer in Scotland, from meaning what the speaker chooses it to mean which, very likely, is not quite what the listener understands by it.

Emmanuel de Martonne, the great French geographer, states with much authority that, locally, the term is traditionally confined to 'the mountains that stand out against the north-western skyline as one surveys the panorama visible from the Tour Magne at Nîmes, or from the Peyrou terrace at Montpellier' However, the term is also used as a provincial name to cover the territory of two old Bishoprics: Velay, the seat of which is Le Puy, and Gévaudan, the seat of which is Mende. This is what Stevenson meant by the Cévennes, and he uses Velay and Gévaudan as chapter headings in *Travels with a Donkey*. Sometimes the Cévennes are held to include the great limestone plateaus called the Causses, but the Cévennes proper are mountains made up of crystalline rocks.

As RLS quickly observed, the Cévennes are very like the Highlands of Scotland. A difference in latitude means that, although they are higher – you begin, as it were, at the height of Ben Lomond – they are not hills where there is permanent snow, but the highest summits are close to it. There are successive ridges of relatively undistinguished hills with shapely exceptions. There are game birds and hawks, and adders constitute a threat to the rambler who is not paying attention. They are glorious where there are natural woods, and tolerable where there are plantations as are the Scottish Highlands. The greatest resemblance is, however, in their mountain rivers which have the air of Highland burns, singing in their rocky green beds, and forming a series of delightful water-breaks. For the Cévennes are above all a heartland for some important rivers of France: the Loire and the Allier, the Lot and the Tarn, for all the quintessentially French images they may conjure up, begin as Highland burns.

De Martonne points out that the drove roads of the Cévennes have long been significant. 'The routes they have followed for centuries are traceable from a distance by the white ribbon they make on the mountainside. These drailles are one of the characteristic features of the landscape in the Cévennes.' It seems almost certain that Stevenson went from place to place by the 'usual route' of the day, by the usual means for a pedestrian. Today he would probably have cycled, or, knowing him, have gone by car; and both of those means of transport are suitable for pilgrims following in his footsteps. Anyone choosing to follow him should obtain either The *Cévennes Journal*, edited by Gordon Golding, or the French translation of *Travels* by Gilbert L'homme, both of which are products of the centenary, and both of which have literary and topographical explanatory notes. The National Park has created a walking route which, where Stevenson's route sticks too well to the tarmac – of which as an 'Engineer' he would undoubtedly have approved – deviates slightly from it without betraying its essential qualities. The map-guide by the Féderation Française de la Randonnée Pédestre is invaluable.

'Modestines' can still be hired. Indeed, one of the more amusing outcomes of the centenary celebrations is that, initially, a single enterprise was set up to exploit the wish of the legitimate successors of Stevenson to have a donkey, but, owing to a dispute, an offshoot arose, and there are now two distinct claimants offering 'Rando avec Ane'. Indeed, a recent visit to the 'Relais Stevenson' disclosed what might have been a Shetland Pony rather than a donkey, masquerading under the trees by the river bank, flicking flies away with its tail. Stevenson would have been delighted by all this.

Stevenson is present, but unobtrusive. He is most evident between Le Monastier and St Jean du Gard at Club Stevenson, a night-club and horse-riding establishment near Pradelles, and the Relais Stevenson between Florac and Cassagnas. The latter is a former railway station on a line which has come and gone since Stevenson's day, now a wayside restaurant. A close approximation to the route – in some respects more faithful to Stevenson – can be followed by car.

Le Monastier itself, with its abbey church and castle, museum and memorial, will be the starting point for pilgrims following in Stevenson's footsteps. In the four weeks he spent there RLS wrote parts of *New Arabian Nights* and *Edinburgh: Picturesque Notes*. As readers of *Travels* will recall, his landlady was Madame Morel, whose hôtel was in the Place de la Fromagerie. The Edinburgh literary topographer, R.T. Skinner, noticed her death in the *Scotsman* in 1931:

> Stevenson, she stated, was an early riser; he made breakfast for himself – eggs, milk, rum. In the morning he went for a walk over the hills or descended to the stream which he loved most dearly, and which he could hear at night 'go singing down the valley' till he fell asleep. The afternoon was generally. 'I sketch,' he wrote home to his mother, 'I shoot with the revolver, I work, I take long walks; generally I have a good time; above all I am happy to meet none but strangers.' At night he preferred to write at the table of the dining-hall, as a rule retiring early.

We know a good deal about the time which RLS spent in Le Monastier:

> "The country is beautiful, rather too like the Highlands, but not so grand. The valley of the Gazielle below the village is my favourite spot; a winding dell of cliffs and firwoods with here and there green meadows. The Mézenc, highest point of central France, is only a few miles from here."

He struck up an acquaintanceship with a highway engineer 'a fellow from the Ponts et Chaussées', to whom he gave a 'walk-on' part in *The Treasure of Franchard.* RLS accompanied him, on occasion, further afield. He describes one walk to the borders of the Vivarais, which sounds as if it might have taken him to the foot of Mont Mézenc, and which, we know, exhausted him:

> As far as the eye can reach, one swelling line of hill-tops rises and falls behind another; and if you climb an eminence, it is only to see new and farther ranges behind these.

However, he seems to have generally confined himself to the immediate locality, but we can be fairly sure, for example, that he reached the charming château de Vacherès, a little distance from Le Monastier. He visited Laussonne, the next village a few kilometres away, indeed he made it the subject of some of his sketches. He makes an interesting reference to George Sand, whose novels he had read eagerly:

> There, at Laussonne, George Sand spent a day while she was gathering materials for the Marquis de Villemer [1860]; and I have spoken with an old man who was then a child running about the inn kitchen, and who still remembers her with a sort of reverence. It appears that he spoke French imperfectly; for this reason George Sand chose him for a companion, and whenever he let slip a broad and picturesque phrase in patois, she would make him repeat it again and again till it was graven on her memory. The word for a frog particularly pleased her fancy; and it would be curious to know if she afterwards employed it in her works. The peasants, who knew nothing of letters and had never so much as heard of local colour, could not explain her chattering with this backward child; and to them she seemed a very homely lady and far from beautiful; the most famous man-killer of the age appealed so little to Velaisian swineherds!

There is a characteristic touch in RLS's departure, related by Skinner:

> With tears in her eyes, the French lady, whose death is announced, used to tell how Stevenson, in quitting their village, recompensed royally the various domestics, and kissed everybody connected with her establishment.

Early highlights of the journey include the crossing of the Loire at Goudet and the view of the infant river from Beaufort Castle, and the Lac du Bouchet, a circular volcanic lake where one realises, because of the fuss made of a rather ordinary stretch of water, how few natural lakes there are in France, and where the very Auberge where Stevenson stayed can be seen. Le Bouchet is on the watershed between the Loire and the Allier, the upper valley of which is now followed for some considerable distance. Langogne is a bustling town with attractive remnants of its medieval core. Near the town is the Naussac Reservoir, a spectacular change since 1878.

Between Langogne and Luc Stevenson left the Allier and got lost. Paradoxically, this stretch may be the least altered ordinary part of the route, to be recommended to latter day followers in Stevenson's footsteps, of which our man said 'Why anyone should desire to go to Cheylard or to Luc is more than my much inventing spirit can embrace'. His description of the terrain holds good today:

> I was soon out of the cultivated basin of the Allier, and away from the ploughing oxen and such like sights of the country. Moor and heathery marsh, tracts of rock and pines, little woods of birch jewelled with autumn yellow, here and there a few naked cottages and bleak fields, these were the character of the country. Hill and valley followed valley and hill; little green and stony cart tacks wandered in and out of one another, split into three or four, died away in marshy places, began again sporadically on a hillside and, above all on the borders of a wood. I used to have a far better hand for locality than I have, but even at my best, I question whether I could have made a good thing of this intermittent labyrinth.

The district can be explored by using the train between Luc and Langogne. The footpaths are still as perplexing in spite of the best efforts of the paint-daubers. It was in this section, the edges of the Forest of Mercoire, that, before Stevenson's day, the Beast Of Gévaudan, 'the Napoleon Bonaparte of Wolves', terrorised the countryside from 1764 to 1767. Travellers of a nervous disposition might wish to avoid it, just in case. Sleepy Luc is dominated by a huge statue of the Virgin which rather overwhelms some interesting castle ruins. This statue was erected in the very year, 1878, that Stevenson passed Luc, and he makes mention of it.

Next is the rebuilt monastery of Notre-Dame-des-Neiges which caught fire in 1912, not that it had been in existence very long when RLS got there, having been built in 1850. At La Bastide, a railway junction, the Paris-Nîmes line crosses the Cévennes by a tunnel at their lowest point, and a branch railway line to Mende accompanies the now tiny Allier. This is followed as far as Chasseradès. Stevenson was forced to spend an uncomfortable night lodging with the navvies, engaged in the construction of the line, who had filled up the inn. A short distance away a rivulet called the Chassezac, now crossed by a fine viaduct at Mirandol, under construction when RLS was there, flows in the opposite direction from the Allier towards the Mediterranean. Then comes the Montaigne de Goulet, separating the Allier and the infant Lot, and Mont Lozère, the highest of the Cévennes, separating the Lot and the Tarn, which was the scene of 'the night among the Pines'. RLS reached the Tarn, here a brawling mountain river, at Pont de Montvert.

This attractive mountain village is on the threshold of the country of the Camisards. It has the best bridge left on the route, and the most charming stretch of river, together with a comprehensive ecological museum. A distinguishing feature, even today, of the villages of the Cévennes is that, in addition to the little notice board announcing the times of masses, there is another stating the times of the Protestant services. These hills, like the Uplands of the British Isles, provided a refuge at times of religious persecution, and successive groups of Protestants in France made their homes there. The independent peasants of the Cévennes fought hard, after the Revocation of the Edict of Nantes, to maintain their religion in a series of wars which began in 1702. This was an important attraction of the area for Stevenson who perceived himself as a rebel, and something of an expert on the Scottish Covenanters. In the following passage in his *Cévennes Journal* written in Florac, a little place he liked very much, he illuminates the reception he got on his travels, and makes the parallel with Scotland explicit:

> Everyone had some suggestion for my guidance; and the sub-prefectorial map was fetched from the sub-prefecture itself, and much thumbed among coffee cups and glasses of liqueur. Most of these kind advisors were Protestant, though I observed that Protestant and Catholic intermingled in a very easy manner; and it surprised me to see what a lively memory still subsisted of the religious war. Among the hills of the South West, by Mauchline, Cumnock or Carsphairn, in isolated farms or in the manse, serious Presbyterian people still recall the days of the great persecution, and the graves of local martyrs are still piously regarded. But in towns and among the so-called better classes I fear that these doings have become an idle tale.

Stevenson followed the valley of the Tarn from Pont de Montvert to Florac which stands at the head of the limestone Gorges of the Tarn, a tourist attraction subject nowadays to some of French tourism's more blatant manifestations, where one is charged, for example, to see the most striking view. However, above Florac the 'Scottish' river is quiet and delightful, as is another tributary, the Mimette, which provided the écrivain écossais with his next route into the hills. About Florac the motorist can follow the author more closely than the modern rambler who is taken by more suitable mountain tracks across the next two ridges. The next watershed, which he crossed near Mont Mars brought him, as he pointed out, to the Mediterranean Lands:

> I was now on the separation of two vast watersheds; behind me all the streams were bound for the Garonne and the Western Ocean; before me was the watershed of the Rhône. You make take this ridge as lying at the heart of the country of the Camisards.

Just beyond the ridge, at Plan de Fontmort, is a prominent obelisk, erected in 1887 to commemorate the centenary of the Edict of Tolerance signed by Louis XVI which brought to an end the struggle in the Cévennes. It would certainly have been included in Stevenson's itinerary had it been put up earlier, because it marks 'the heart of the country of the Camisards'. RLS wrote a poem about Jean Cavalier (1680-1740), the Camisard chief whose *Memoirs* he read, but he excluded it from both *Travels* and *Underwoods*. It begins:

> These are your hills, John Cavalier.
> Your father's kids you tended here,
> And grew, among these mountains wild,
> A humble and religious child.
> Fate turned the wheel; you grew and grew;
> Bold Marshals doffed the hat to you
> God whispered counsels in your ear
> To guide your sallies, Cavalier.

This ridge nearly finished Modestine; the next col did. It is the last ridge of the Cévennes that RLS crossed, and he hurried up it as night fell, knowing it would provide him with a good view. He saw the distant ridges by moonlight from the Col de Saint-Pierre. At the col is a milestone – a waymarker from another age – indicating the Route Royale from St Flour to Nîmes and, at the summit of Mont Saint Pierre, a short delightful walk away through birch and chestnut woods, there is an admirable view indicator. From it Mont Aigoual, the isolated mountain mass, which formed an important retreat for the 'Maquis' during the Second World War, can be seen. It fired Stevenson's imagination because it also formed a stronghold for a Protestant hero, André Castanet.

Col de St Pierre: the final col crossed by RLS

The pass winds down to St Jean du Gard where Stevenson parted from Modestine. You can visit the museum there, too, and, in the main street, see the ring in a doorway to which Modestine was finally hitched. Stevenson was saddened, but he hurried off to Alais in a diligence to catch a train. He was anxious to find out who had written to him, Poste Restante.

Stevenson in France: Provence

I was only happy once, and that was at Hyères. [RLS (1891)]

I live in a most sweet corner of the universe, sea and fine hills before me and a rich variegated plain; and at my back a craggy hill, loaded with vast feudal ruins. I am very quiet; a person passing by my door half startles me; but I enjoy the most aromatic airs, and at night the most wonderful view into a moonlit garden. By day this garden fades into nothing, overpowered by its surroundings and the luminous distance; but at night and when the moon is out, that garden, the arbour, the flight of stairs that mount the artificial hillock, the plumed blue gum trees, that hang trembling, become the very skirts of Paradise. [RLS to Will Low (1883)]

Stevenson and his wife spent much of the period between October, 1882 and July, 1884 in Provence. Provence, like the 'Highlands of Scotland', is a rather elastic term, but it certainly includes Marseilles and Hyères; whether it comprehends Montpellier, or the Côte d'Azur, or not, can be debated, but it is not used here to describe Menton, for example. RLS was not well, and, at least twice, he was seriously ill; and, he never found a completely satisfactory place to live. However, although it was small, and so cramped that they were unable to entertain visitors, he was delighted with the tiny chalet which they eventually located in Hyères. Throughout he corresponded vigorously with his family and with his friends and, when he could work, he produced a great deal of interest. Indeed, as a writer, he was engaged

La Solitude: the chalet – from the Paris Exhibition – taken for 18 months by the Stevensons

both in creative work, and in the rewarding business of getting work into print. It was his most fertile period in France.

To begin with, he and his cousin Bob sought a place in Montpellier, but he was unwell there, and a Doctor advised him not to stay. He therefore went to Marseilles, where Fanny joined him, and they identified a suitable house to rent in an overgrown industrial village, not far from the city. At first the Campagne Defli, San Marcel seemed ideal – this is Van Gogh country with imposing limestone outcrops to alleviate dusty plains – but it proved to be damp, and when there was an outbreak of fever Stevenson went to Nice, leaving Fanny to pack. There was then a series of misadventures during the course of which Fanny said she believed him to be dead. In fact he was unwell, and letters and a telegram had gone astray.

They were re-united in Marseilles, and returned to Nice until RLS had recovered. In February 1883 they went to stay in Hyères at the Hôtel des Iles d'Or and, in March, rented La Solitude, a chalet in the Swiss style, part of a job lot purchased by the owner of the estate from the Paris Exhibition of 1878, at which, ironically, RLS had been, technically at least, a functionary. The character of the chalet can still be appreciated, although, understandably, it has been extended and rebuilt. However, there are sufficient hints in nearby buildings in the present Rue Victor Basch to suggest what it was like. The Stevenson chalet has a plaque. What was clearly its principal recommendation was its garden, still, evidently, a delight to its owners. Before the name was changed, the chalet was in the 'Road of the Falling Stone', a road which climbs steeply towards the castle above Hyères. It was, one has to say, a decidedly odd place for two semi-invalids to choose to live, unless they were optimists, as the Stevensons, without much justification, undoubtedly were.

The road which links Victor Basch with the Avenue des Iles d'Or is now named after a regular literary visitor to Hyères, the American novelist, Edith Wharton (1867-1937). A statue now commemorates the great French historian Jules Michelet (1798-1874) who was one of Stevenson's particular favourites. He died in the resort.

Hyères is the oldest of France's 'Mediterranean' resorts. The focal point is the resort town of Hyères les Palmiers (an address which RLS generally carefully wrote out in full) which is, in fact, some distance from the shores of the great southern European sea, and separated from it by mosquito-ridden lagoons. The palm trees are certainly very striking, some over 30m in height. Cook's *Travellers' Handbook* states 'The eucalypti globuli are unrivalled in Europe. Yuccas, araucaria Bidwilla, pittersporum, dracena, agavi of every variety, aralia, bamboo, magnolia, all grow in the open air. Hyères is a paradise for butterfly collectors.' However, the place had some disadvantages: it was exposed to the Mistral at times, it was on a branch line, and the old town was considered, by Stevenson's fellow-Scot, Miller, to be very dirty and badly drained. It is unsurprising that other places usurped its pre-eminence. However, Hyères had two indisputable assets: its 'Saracen' castle, airily situated above the town, and, just off the coast, some islands, the Iles d'Hyères [d'Or], to relieve the infinities of the blue blue sea.

The Iles d'Or are undoubtedly very worthy islands indeed, and the view of them from the town, let alone the possibility of reaching them from one of its satellites, may well account for the reputation of Hyères. RLS had an offer from an American publisher to write a book about the Greek Islands, but Colvin reports that it was a book which Stevenson did not write. It was conjectured at Hyères, perhaps overlooking Porquerolles, where their thoughts turned to the islands of the Ionian Sea, and the comparison between them, and RLS's beloved Hebrides. Colvin observed shrewdly that Stevenson could not work much in libraries, and lacked, in this instance, 'a Greek scholar's special enthusiasm':

> We ran over the blunt monosyllabic names of some of the Hebridean group – Coll, Mull, Eigg, Rum, Muck, and Skye – and contrasted them with the euphonious Greek names…We speculated on a book written that should try to strike the several notes of these twin island regions, of their scenery, inhabitants, and traditions, of Greek and Gaelic lay and legend, and the elements of Homeric and Ossianic poetry. [Sidney Colvin *Memories and Notes of Persons and Places* 1913]

The Castle of Hyères, an enceinte, 200m above sea level, was first erected in the seventh century. The ruins, mere vestiges of the past, but very atmospheric, and not very far above the Stevensons' house, are well-worth exploring on their own account, and for the splendid views of the interior, as well as of the Mediterranean. It can be noted that one of the old churches is dedicated to St. Louis.

The Iles d'Or Hotel is, today, an apartment block. Since the chalet was so small, it was where the Stevensons had their visitors stay. For example, they were visited by Colvin in April, 1883; and, later, by Charles Baxter and W.E. Henley in January, 1884. They spent a week there, and then went with our hero to Nice. These two were both good for him – Baxter was one of his great cronies during his youth, and Henley, a friend whom he had made later, but one who had taken to RLS and his circle as if he had been there from the beginning – and bad for him, because their company probably over-excited RLS. In Nice he was taken seriously ill, and did not recover, even partially, until March when he returned to La Solitude.

The coterie of friends who visited Hyères would undoubtedly have included James Walter Ferrier, had it been possible. He died tragically young in September, 1883, and this first death of a beloved contemporary affected the young author deeply. Stevenson, Baxter and Ferrier were probably as dissolute as one another in their youth, but Ferrier was vulnerable to alcoholism. On hearing of his death RLS wrote to his sister, and what he said to her suggested a moving essay, *Old Mortality* which he later published [in May 1884] with her permission. To their great delight she came out to Hyères in late March, 1884.

Coggie Ferrier, grand-daughter of John Wilson [Christopher North], is described by Mrs E.M. Sellar in her *Recollections and Impressions*: "She has inherited much of her mother [Margaret Anne Wilson]'s wild wit and, perhaps somewhat reckless humour and wonderful powers of mimicry. All this is known and appreciated by those who have met her even in the most casual manner, but only those who are most intimate with her know what a heart of gold she has, and what capacity for sacrificing herself for the good of a friend."

Coggie brought Edinburgh to Hyères. Both Stevenson and his wife derived much support from her presence. Among her accomplishments was an ability to sing Scottish songs well, and it was she who sang *The Skye Boat Song* to Stevenson in Bournemouth. In Hyères she read *Thrawn Janet* to the delight of its author.

Work undertaken by Stevenson in Provence included finishing The *Silverado Squatters*, helping Fanny to devise tales published as *More New Arabian Nights*, then re-starting *Prince Otto* which his letters were full of from April, 1883 onwards. Shortly afterwards he heard that *Treasure Island*, written in parts, was to be published as a book. He also worked up the article for Henley's magazine about Fontainebleau, and another about Realism. He also embarked on another part-novel, *The Black Arrow*. In the summers of both 1883 and 1884 they went from Hyères to Royat, where some of his 'Hyères' work was continued.

His spells of illness enabled him to complete *A Child's Garden of Verses*. When he was unwell (and in one case unsighted) he could not write at length, but he did find creative occupation in these deceptively simple poems. They were begun in Braemar, inspired by Kate Greenaway, continued in Nice, and concluded in Hyères and Royat. He thought them to be trifles, but they had sufficient quality to last, and are among his best known verses.

The poem in *Underwoods* entitled *To a Gardener* evokes Hyères:

> Friend, in my mountain-side demesne,
> My plain-beholding, rosy, green
> And linnet-haunted garden-ground,
> Let still the esculents abound.

Another poem which seems to have originated there was *The Canoe Speaks* which he sent to Low from La Solitude with the idea that the American might illustrate it for an American magazine. The poem, already quoted, relates to their time together in Fontainebleau. It was not published until he included it in *Underwoods* [1887]. What is, perhaps, his best known single poem, *Requiem*, is dated 'Hyères May 1884', but Janet Adam Smith points out that there were previous versions, and variations:

Under the wide and starry sky,
Dig the grave and let me die.
Glad did I live and gladly die,
And I laid me down with a will.
This be the verse you grave for me:
"Here he lies where he longed to be;
Home is the sailor, home from sea,
And the hunter home from the hill.

However, Stevenson had intimations of mortality often enough, and the poem fits in with a rather whimsical epitaph he wrote for himself at Hyères. He sent it from Hyères to Colvin in November, 1883, to whom he had sent the original epitaph in *Requiem*:

Here lies
The carcase
of
Robert Louis Stevenson
An active, austere, and not inelegant
writer,
who,
at the termination of a long career,
wealthy, wise, benevolent, and honoured by
the attention of two hemispheres,
yet owned it to have been his crowning favour
TO INHABIT
LA SOLITUDE

(With the consent of the intelligent edility [magistrates] of Hyères, he has been interred, below this frugal stone, in the garden which he honoured for so long with his poetic presence.)

Perhaps, so far as France is concerned, Stevenson is interred in Hyères.

Stevenson and Royat

Stevenson visited Royat-les-Bains in July and August, 1883 and, again, in June and July, 1884. His sojourns in Royat ought to receive more attention than they sometimes do, although Royat cannot be considered as significant as several other places in France in the story of his life. However, he was there as long as he was in the Cévennes, and longer than he was on the Sambre and Meuse, which inspired his Inland Voyage, and almost as protractedly as he was in the Forest of Fontainebleau, or in Paris. Royat forms a part of Stevenson's 'Hyères Period' which extended from March 1883 until June 1884, but it is sufficiently distinctive to be treated separately.

Some mineral waters were alleged, from time to time, to be efficacious in the treatment of certain forms of TB, although in most cases, including Stevenson's, it was more a matter of spa towns providing a suitable environment for complete rest. Needless to say resorts vied with one another in emphasising the suitability of their waters, and of their situation for the treatment of invalids, and patients sometimes made long journeys at great expense in search of doubtful remedies. Stevenson could not be described as quite falling into that category.

Royat was one of a succession of watering places which Stevenson, and his wife, who was something of an invalid herself, tried. It is situated near Clermont Ferrand and nowadays forms part of it, but in Stevenson's day it was a separate place. The little resort still has the delightful atmosphere of its nineteenth century self, and the higher regard in which the French hold such cures to this day mean that its elements as a spa town have been maintained and up-dated. The waters were known to the Romans, but, between 1823 and 1882, the resort underwent a period of rapid development, under the patronage, after 1862, of the Empress Eugénie. The old village of Royat is situated on a hill, dominated by an impressive fortified Romanesque church, an important attraction of itself. The modern spa was laid out at the foot of the hill in the rather narrow valley of the precipitous Tiretaine burn which tumbles through the place in a succession of charming waterfalls. In addition to the Etablissement Thermal and the springs, in a splendidly laid out park, there was a theatre and concert hall together with a casino. One guide noted that with the presence of two regiments of artillery at Clermont, with a permanent band, the standard of orchestral music in the resort was good, and the number of eminent singers who found its waters soothing, meant that concerts reached a very high standard indeed.

When the Stevensons left Hyères in 1883 they went first to Vichy, which they did not care for, and it was Fanny Stevenson, and her son Lloyd Osbourne, who discovered 'the enchanting little watering-place' of Royat. The first year they stayed briefly in the Hotel de la Poste in Clermont Ferrand, then in the Hotel de Lyon in Royat. The second time, in 1884, Stevenson wrote: 'We are at Chabassière's, for of course it was nonsense to go up the hill when we could not walk.' M. Chabassière was an entrepreneur who owned several Hotels in Royat: the Continental seems the most likely. RLS detected, in the little spa town, echoes of Edinburgh:

422. ROYAT — L'Hôtel Continental

Royat: Hôtel Continental

'...there is a note among the chimney pots which suggests Howe Street...'

The granitic plateau and volcanic hills of the Auvergne are said to have more than five hundred distinct mineralised springs, and Royat is one of two or three of the most important resorts. It is situated on the edge of the most spectacular volcanic hills, called Puys, of the Auvergne. The best known of these hills, the Puy de Dôme, is not very far away, and there are numerous sisters, cousins and aunts, lesser Puys, in the neighbourhood. One of the attractions of Royat was the Grotte de Chien, so called, it is said, because it emanates carbon dioxide which, close to the ground, will asphyxiate a dog. Four of the five sources in Royat are warm, vigorous and richly mineralised, and we have, from Fanny Stevenson, a good account of the baths, as she and Stevenson experienced them:

> The baths were more or less arsenical; some so strongly impregnated that they were dangerous, and only given out to drink, in limited quantities, by virtue of the doctor's prescription. One source had a flavour that reminded you of weak chicken broth, and another effervesced, when you plunged into it like champagne.

> There were two ways to reach the baths from our hotel; we might choose an exceedingly steep street, or go more directly down an immense flight of precipitous stairs. As it was our stately, though uncomfortable, custom to be carried in sedan chairs, we generally went by way of the street. There had already been accidents on the stairs; should a bearer slip or lose his hold the consequences would be disastrous. It was against the law for chairs to be taken down the stairs; but if the bearers had several fares in view they were very apt to ignore the regulation. When you ordered a chair, unless ordinary directions were given, it was brought into your bedroom. You stepped inside, usually in your dressing-gown; the door was closed and the curtains drawn until you arrived at your destination, where you alighted in front of your bath-tub. The privacy was absolute and the discomfort extreme. As you could not see out, you were always nervously uncertain what route your bearer had taken, and you might unexpectedly find yourself in the middle of the forbidden stairs. The air space was limited, and in warm weather the interior of the chair became very stuffy. There were two bearers to each chair, who went at a jog-trot, purposely refraining from keeping step, which would swing their burden from side to side. The uneven movement gave a jolting effect that was the most tiring thing imaginable. [Prefatory Note to *Black Arrow*]

When they were there in 1883 RLS was reasonably well, and he and Fanny wrote enthusiastically to Stevenson's parents about the resort and Thomas and Margaret Stevenson, the lighthouse engineer and his wife, joined them.

That summer in Royat is of considerable interest in respect of Stevenson's development both as a person, and as a writer. Stevenson's father was

LE JEUNE HOMME PUT APERCEVOIR UN GARÇON
QUI SE GLISSAIT HORS DE LA SALLE....

Black Arrow

distinguished in his own right, and was greatly disappointed when his son did not follow in his footsteps, or in those of his even more famous grandfather, Robert Stevenson, and become an engineer. He was decidedly uncertain about his son's chosen profession, that of writer; yet he had, until then, subsidised it. Richard Aldington, in *Portrait of a Rebel*, has described his attitude as 'a strange mixture of tenderness and tyranny, good will and misunderstanding.' At this time *Treasure Island*, which had been published as a serial in a magazine, was with its publishers in book form. He was also at work on *A Child's Garden of Verses*. These were two of the works which were to give him, eventually, a reputation probably greater than that of his illustrious grandfather, Robert Stevenson.

Fanny noted that it was evident to them that Thomas Stevenson's health was beginning to fail. Thereafter it seems to have been the son who was in the ascendancy in relationships between them. However, the family seem to have got on well at Royat. The disputes between father and son were forgotten, and Thomas Stevenson, who was always assiduous in correcting his son's work and making suggestions for improvements to it, contributed in this way to the story he was presently engaged upon.

This was *The Black Arrow*, inspired by *The Paston Letters*, a documentary record of an English family at the time of the Wars of the Roses. He had begun it as a serial story at the request of the Editor of *Young Folks* who published *Treasure Island*. It was a swashbuckling tale set in medieval England, of which Stevenson himself had no high opinion. He left Hyères in a hurry, and had gone first to Marseilles, by stages to Vichy, and thence to Royat; he thus lost the thread of the story, and had to await the arrival of his proofs before being able to continue it. Parts of it followed him round France. Stevenson's charm and generosity of spirit is illustrated by the fact that, when, even so, the proof reader at *Young Folks* had to point out to him some inconsistencies in the resolution of the plot, RLS praised him and the quality of his work generally, rather than being churlish about such an intervention, as some authors might have been.

Further interest attaches to *The Black Arrow*, completed during his first summer at Royat. When it was serialised in America, it was very successful. It was illustrated by RLS's friend Will Low, the American painter whom he had first met in Paris, who married a Frenchwoman, and settled for some years in France. The story was, too, one of the first literary projects which interested the famous French critic, Marcel Schwob, who sought permission to translate it. In spite of RLS's low opinion of it, the young readers of his story liked it, and a famous British historian, G. M. Trevelyan, praised its authenticity. Another Francophile, D. B. Wyndham-Lewis wrote about it in the foreword to his book on François Villon:

On this day before this book floated into my mind, I had been wandering down the Rue St. Jacques, the docte Rue St. Jacques, and over the Petit-Pont, as I had often done before, repeating the verses of this poet, whom I have revered since my boyhood when I first lighted on Robert Louis Stevenson's essay, evoked (as will easily be remembered) by the great biographical study of François Villon by Auguste Longnon. Of Stevenson's essay I still think with gratitude; and indeed it must be acknowledged as the best study of the medieval world (with *The Black Arrow*) ever put on paper by a nineteenth-century Calvino-Agnostic. From the day of reading it I became eager for more of this poet...

It was from Royat that Stevenson wrote to the French inn-keeper whom he knew in California, Jules Simoneau, giving his appraisal of the relative merits of the English and the French:

...their merits and defects make a balance:

The English	*The French*
hypocrites	free from hypocrisy
good, stout reliable friends	incapable of friendship
dishonest to the root	fairly honest
fairly decent to women	rather indecent to women

Stevenson also set a short story called *The Enchantress* in Royat. The long-lost story, written in the South Seas, was only recently published. It begins with a gambler who has lost all his money in the Casino who encounters a mysterious woman. Stevenson generally wrote about places at a distance. This story, however slight it is, confirms that memories of Royat resurfaced when RLS was in the South Seas. Here he describes a moonlit walk:

We walked on in silence up the hill road; as we went the moon began to peer at intervals out of rifts among the clouds, and to shed flying glimpses on the Limagne and the towered city of Clermont at our feet. Presently she came to a wider island of clear sky, and her light fell now steadily around us.

The spa was the last place in which RLS spent a considerable period in France. When he was in the South Seas, Stevenson imagined himself returning to Royat, and receiving visits from his friends. He had an affection for the place.

Some Concluding Remarks

Dr Jekyll and Mr Hyde was published in 1886, the year of Stevenson's last visit to Paris. Although *Treasure Island*, which did a great deal for his reputation, was published in book form while he was in France, RLS was, during the years when he knew France, a relatively obscure Scotsman who wrote a great deal, rather than a famous author. However, his French pieces included his most successful travel-books, several highly skilful essays, in *Prince Otto*, a stylish, if ultimately unsuccessful novel, and several of his most interesting poems. RLS never was a dramatist, nor was his collaborator, Henley, but their best known piece *Deacon Brodie* was produced during that time. The elements of RLS's greatness were evident when he was in France, and there can be no doubt that France made a highly significant contribution to them.

Nothing delighted Stevenson more than to receive, in Sydney in 1890, a letter from the young French essayist and critic, Marcel Schwob (1867-1905). Schwob had written enthusiastically to RLS when he was embarking on his own career, saying how much he admired the Scottish author's work. Stevenson replied enthusiastically:

> Comprehend how I have lived much of my time in France, and loved your country, and many of its people, and all the time was learning that which your country has to teach – breathing in rather that atmosphere of art which can only there be breathed; and all the time knew – and raged to know – that I might write with the pen of angels or of heroes, and no Frenchman be the least the wiser! And now steps in

M. Marcel Schwob, writes me the most kind encouragement, and reads and understands, and is kind enough to like my work.

Gazetteer of Literary Sites in France Associated with RLS

[CD] Diary kept by Alison Cunningham of the Stevenson family's visit to France in 1863.

[L] Letters

ALAIS [ALES], Gard. Attractive chief town of an arrondisement of Gard, on the Gardon. RLS wrote from there to Colvin at the end of his *Travels with a Donkey.*

AMIENS, Somme. In 1863 the 12 year-old RLS made his first acquaintance with a French town in Amiens where the family stayed overnight at the Hôtel du Rhin. 'Cummy' found log fires odd! [CD] Paul Bourget whom RLS discovered in Sydney was born there.

AUTUN, Saône-et-Loire. P.G. Hamerton (1834-94), the poet, artist and critic who started *Portfolio,* in which RLS's 'Roads' appeared, moved eventually to La Tuilerie, Autun. He was one of the first critics to recognise Stevenson's potential for greatness. RLS paid him a speculative visit there when he was returning to Paris from Alais in 1878; a visit which both of them greatly appreciated. Hamerton shared RLS's interest in canoeing, and proposed a joint cruise down the Rhône; neither of them achieved this ambition. To Stendhal (1783-1842) the town of Autun was 'one of the most curious in France.'

AVIGNON, Vaucluse. Famous city on the Rhône, visited by RLS in Nov. 1873 when he was 'ordered South'. The philosopher John Stuart Mill died in Avignon in that year. RLS wrote with great enthusiasm about it in a letter. He particularly liked the magnificent panorama from the hill near the Castle and the feel of the south:

"The hills seemed just fainting into the sky; even the great peak above Carpentras [Mont Ventoux] (Lord knows how many metres above the sea) seemed unsubstantial and thin in the breadth and the potency of the sunshine."

Many years later Andrew Lang wanted RLS, half a world away from him, to tell an adventure story:

"In turning over old Jacobite pamphlets, I found a forgotten romance of Prince Charles's hidden years, and longed that Mr Stevenson should retell it. There was a treasure, an authentic treasure; there were real spies, a real assassin; a real, or reported, rescue of a lovely girl from a fire in Strasbourg by the Prince. The tale was to begin sur le pont d'Avignon: a young Scotch exile watching the Rhône, thinking how much of it he could cover with a salmon fly, thinking of the Tay or Beauly. To him enter another shady tramping exile, Blairthwaite, the murderer. And so it was to run on, as the author's fancy might lead him, with Alan Breck and the Master for characters." [*Adventures Among Books*]

BASTIDE, La. see Cévennes

BLÉYMARD, Le. see Cévennes

BLÉRANCOURT, Aisne. The Château houses the Franco-American Museum where paintings by Harrison and Robinson, American painters whom RLS met at Fontainebleau hang.

BOULOGNE-SUR-MER, Pas-de-Calais. RLS used this crossing on his return from Germany with Sir Walter Simpson in September, 1872, and wrote an amusing verse letter to Chas Baxter which begins:

Blame me not that this epistle
Is the first you have from me.
Idleness has held me fettered,
But at last the times are bettered

And once more I wet my whistle
Here in France, beside the sea.

Sainte-Beuve, the critic whose work RLS found sympathetic, was born there.

CALAIS, Pas de Calais. When the 1863 Party [CD] reached Calais Thomas Stevenson considered the Channel too rough to cross, so they stayed the night.

CANNES, Alpes Maritimes. The 1863 Party [CD] spent two nights at the Hôtel du Nord; the 1864 Party returned by way of Cannes.

CERNAY-LA-VILLE, Yvelines. Significant artists' colony which RLS visited with his cousin Bob, and alone. Presided over by 'the admirable Pelouse' whose friends and admirers erected a statue to him beyond the waterfalls. (see Fontainebleau)

CHATEAU RENARD, Loiret. see Fontainebleau

CHATILLON-SUR-LOIRE, Loiret. Scene of RLS's imprisonment. (see Fontainebleau)

CHATILLON-SUR-LOING, Loiret. see Fontainebleau

COMPIÈGNE, Oise. One of Stevenson's French literary heroes, Dumas (père), regularly and rumbustiously stayed at the Hôtel de la Cloche. RLS was very taken with the Town Hall clock, 'with three little mechanical figures, each one with a hammer in his hand, whose business it is to chime the hours', and with the architecture of the Town Hall: "It is a monument of Gothic insecurity, all turreted, and gargoyled, and slashed, and bedizened with half a score of architectural fancies."

COUCY-LE-CHATEAU, Aisne. Superb fortified hill-town with a splendid C13 castle which RLS saw from the top of the tower of the Cathedral in Noyon.

CREIL, Oise. Stopping place on the 'Inland Voyage', where RLS commented particularly on a girls' boarding school; and on the 'nondescript' church with 'a faithful model of a canal-boat' in the vault. RLS reflected on Catholicism and indulgences.

DIEPPE, Seine Maritime. The Newhaven-Dieppe crossing between

London and Paris is the most direct, combining a longer sea journey with two relatively short railway journeys; it was the way the fashionable traveller went. On New Year's Day, 1878 RLS was busy trying to get his first book finished at the Hôtel des Étrangers in Dieppe. He wrote to Colvin full of uncertainty: "I should not feel such a muff as I do, if I once saw the thing in boards with a ticket on its back." [L]

DIJON, Côte d'Or. RLS lunched at Dijon on his journey South in 1863. [CD]

FLORAC. see Cévennes

FONTAINEBLEAU. see Text

FÈRE, La, Aisne. A garrison town when RLS visited it during the 'Inland Voyage'. They were turned away from the best inn, but well-received in a humbler one. The landlady's rudeness at the former earned the chapter heading 'La Fère of Cursed Memory'.

GIEN, Loiret. In the centre an impressive castle of Charlemagne's is now a museum. RLS reached the Loire here on his tramp through the Gâtinais.

GOUDET, Haute-Loire. see Cévennes

Hyères: Grand Hôtel des Iles d'Or

48 HYÈRES. — *Grand Hôtel des Iles d'Or.* — LL.

HYÈRES, Var. Places to visit include Chalet la Solitude, Rue Victor Basch. The road was, in RLS's time called the Boulevard de la Pierre Glissante, the road of the sliding stone: not the best place for an invalid to choose. His house has been substantially altered, but the hall nearby gives the flavour of it, and the garden retains its charm. The house has an appropriate plaque. The Hôtel Iles d'Or is now a residential block rather than a grand hotel, but it retains its facade. Stevenson stayed there, and billeted his friends, including Henley and Colvin, there. The Château, the vestigial remains of a 'Crusaders' Castle', is interesting because of its situation, and on account of the superb views which Colvin and Stevenson enjoyed of the Iles d'Or. The Musée et Bibliothéque, Place Lefèvre, formerly a railway station, houses the reference library which has a good record of Stevenson; nearby is a statue to Edith Wharton, the American author who also loved Hyères.

LANDRECIES, Nord. Garrison town visited during the 'Inland Voyage'. A sad reminder of the past is that the British War Poet, Wilfred Owen (1893-1918), killed in action at the very end of the Great War is buried in a local cemetery at Ors, nearby.

LANGOGNE, Lozère. see Cévennes

LAUSONNE, Haute Loire. see Cévennes

L'ISLE ADAM, Oise. RLS was mistaken for a day-tripper rather than a seasoned traveller here.

LYON, Rhône. Third city of France. RLS arrived on 8th Jan. 1863 and stayed at the Grand Hôtel Collet. He was taken to see the junction of the Rhône and the Saône. RLS always expressed great affection for the Rhône, and hoped to journey down it. He passed through Lyon several times. [CD] Alphonse Daudet, whom RLS thought the best living French novelist, described his schooldays there in *Le Petit Chose.*

MAUBEUGE, Nord. River-side frontier town where the French part of the 'Inland Voyage' began. RLS had his (customary) difficulties with border officials, related in the book. The present town is industrialised, but evokes past times by the river.

MARSEILLES, Bouches du Rhône. France's second city, which RLS visited briefly several times when in the South of France. The 1863 Party [CD] stayed at the Hôtel des Colonies; in 1883 he was at the

Hôtel du Petit Louvre in the Cannebière, the principal street, where he successfully negotiated the disposal of the lease on Campagne Defli.

MENTON. see Text

MONACO. RLS went there for the Christmas break from Menton in 1873/4, with Colvin and dined with 'the notorious Sir Charles Dilke'. RLS described himself as well pleased with his progress: the two sunbathed under the palm trees. One day they went in a boat to Cap Martin, 'the place of firs and rocks and rosemary.' (see Menton)

MONASTIER, Le see Cévennes

MONTARGIS, Loiret. RLS composed 'A Song of the Road' in the Forest of Montargis in 1878.

MONTE CARLO. "I am sitting on a seat on the low terrace at Monte Carlo; the sea shining in front; on the right old Monaco; on the left Roccabruna, Cap St Martin and the Italian coast; behind me a border full of bees, a wall covered with green creepers and a great clump of palms and aloes." [L Christmas 1873] RLS was not admitted to the Casino, but he told Colvin, who had a distaste for it, that 'it is a very nice Casino, as a Casino...'

MONTIGNY, Seine et Marne. Riverside village on the Loing where W.H. Low lived after he was married.

MONTPELLIER, Hérault. A resort town much in vogue in the early C19, which went rather out of favour. RLS and RAM Stevenson went there in October 1882, but RLS had lung trouble, and it was deemed unsuitable. One can suppose that the place appealed to him because it combined the Cévennes with the Mediterranean; he may have stayed at the Hôtel Nevet. Smollett found Montpellier equally unhealthy in November 1763:

"My asthmatical trouble, which had not given me much disturbance since I left Boulogne, became now very trouble-some, attended with fever, cough, spitting, and lowness of spirits."

MORET, Seine et Marne. Attractive bridge-town where Simpson and the two Stevensons housed the barge. (see Fontainebleau)

MOY, Aisne. see Inland Voyage

NEMOURS. see Fontainebleau

NICE, Alpes Maritimes. The most important Riviera resort. The 1863 Party [CD] spent two weeks there at the Hôtel Chauvain; RLS even attended school there; and went to the Scotch Church [Rue Massena]. He fled to Nice (considered safe from fevers) from St Marcel in late 1882. In Jan. 1884 RLS, Henley and Baxter were in Nice when he was taken seriously ill; he rested in Nice until well enough to return to Hyères. Nice was where he composed 'Penny Whistles' which were included in *A Child's Garden of Verses*. Writing to Baxter earlier he likened the River Phaillon to the Tay, and the rain in Nice to that in Greenock. Fanny relates that "Once in Nice, when exhausted by a long walk, he stopped to rest at a low drinking place. A couple of villainous-looking fellows at the next table ceased speaking, regarded him intently for a few moments, listening to his order, and then resumed their conversation, satisfied that they had nothing to fear. They were discussing their hatred of the English, and the possibility of drugging and robbing the first Englishman who should enter the place."

Marie Bashkirtseff (see Paris) lived in Nice after 1872. Another Scottish literary exile, Tobias Smollett spent 1763/4 in Nice, and was at least partly responsible for inventing it as a seaside resort:

"The people here were much surprised when I began to bathe in the beginning of May. They thought it strange, that a man seemingly consumptive should plunge into the sea, especially when the sea was so cold; and some of the doctors prognosticated immediate death." [*Travels in France & Italy*].

NOYON, Oise. Birthplace of Jean Cauvin [John Calvin] (1509-64). There is now a good museum, but his association with Noyon seems to have escaped RLS. Indeed, he so admired the Cathedral, 'like the poop of some great old battleship', that he avowed that if he ever became a Catholic he would like to be Bishop of Noyon. "I find I never weary of great churches. It is my favourite kind of mountain scenery."

ORANGE, Vaucluse. RLS stayed overnight at this town north of Avignon noted for its Roman ruins. "My first enthusiasm was on rising... and throwing open the shutters. Such a great living flood of sunshine poured in upon me, that I confess to having danced and expressed my satisfaction aloud..."

ORIGNY SAINTE BENOÎTE, Aisne. This industrial village was where RLS flirted with 'three Desdemonas', and the two canoeists saw a manned balloon launched from nearby St Quentin. The place sounds charming in the book, but today it is dominated by a cement works.

PARIS. see Text

PONT-DE-MONTVERT, Lozère. see Cévennes

PONT SAINTE MAXENCE, Oise. In his day this was the site of one of the most elegant triumphs of engineering in Europe: a wafer thin stone arched bridge, but this was unnoticed by RLS.

PONTOISE, Oise. Haunt of Impressionist Painters when RLS was there, but now swamped by Paris. The 'Inland Voyage' ended here, appropriately enough, because neither the Aisne nor the Seine was really suitable for their canoes. They stayed at the Hôtel Grand Cerf, still there.

PONT-SUR-SAMBRE, Aisne. Retains its village atmosphere and sundial as in Stevenson's day, when each town in France kept its own time. The Sambre winds right round the place.

Pont-sur-Sambre:
The clock noted by RLS

Close-up of the plaque showing
local time in Pont-sur-Sambre

PRADELLES, Haute Loire. see Cévennes

PRECY, Oise. "The plain is rich with tufts of poplar. In a wide luminous curve the Oise lay under the hillside." RLS seemed pleased, as he often did, at first, but he went on "The inn is the worst inn in France." The two canoeists went to a bad marionette show there.

PUY, Le, Haute Loire. The spectacular chief town of Haute Loire, and the ancient capital of Velay, situated close to the Loire. RLS arrived in late August 1878, before going to nearby Le Monastier; he found it very attractive and he returned there; on one occasion having a gargantuan breakfast. Notes suggest that he intended to begin *Travels with a Donkey* there.

SENS, Yonne. RLS passed through the town in Nov 1873, and he encountered a blind poet selling his poems in the street. At first he was taken with him, but later decided he lacked style. [L]

ST GERMAIN-DE-CALBERTE, Lozère. see Cévennes

ST GERMAIN-EN-LAYE, Yvelines. RLS and Fanny stayed at the Hôtel du Pavillon Henry IV in 1881 after a week in Paris. "The place pleased us and did us good." They heard a nightingale sing on the terrace of the Château.

St Germain-en-Laye: RLS and Fanny visited the chateau on their brief return to France in 1881

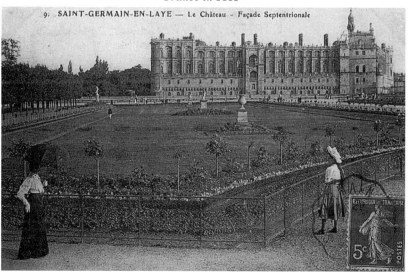

ST JEAN DU GARD, Gard. RLS stayed at the Hôtel du Cheval Blanc. Modestine's subsequent career has been chronicled by the Club Cévenol which has a fine town museum there. (see Cévennes)

ST. MARCEL, Bouches du Rhône. Suburban industrial township on the fringes of Marseilles; RLS and Fanny rented a house there in October, 1882. It was called 'Campagne Defli', and RLS was soon making fun of the name: "It is called Campagne Defli! query Campagne Debug? The Campagne Demosquito goes on here nightly, and is very deadly," he wrote to his cousin, Bob. At first they liked the area, but it proved unsuitable. RLS went to Nice, then Hyères.

TOULON, Var. Naval port visited en route by both the 1863 [CD], and 1864 family parties. Cummy was shocked that the shops were open on a Sunday.

VADENCOURT, Aisne. Village where the Sambre-Oise canal joins the Oise; the scene remains interesting and evocative. It was where the two canoeists launched their vessels into the river swollen by rain.

VICHY, Allier. Noted Spa; the Stevensons did not care for the place. (see Royat)

VILLEFRANCHE, Alpes Maritimes. RLS and his nurse visited this resort in 1863. [CD]

On the Trail of Stevenson in France

The following suggested itinerary visits most of the sites associated with RLS in France. It is a crowded schedule, and it will be found tiring if undertaken in fourteen days.

1. Inland Voyage
Bases: Guise, Compiègne, Laon [two nights]
Visit: Noyon, Blérancourt, Coucy, Vadencourt, and Pont sur Sambre.
Link: [A26] Dijon, Beaune, Autun, Chalons, Lyon; then Le Puy

2. The Cévennes
Bases: Le Puy, Florac, etc. [three nights]
Visit: Le Monastier, Langogne, Le Pont Montvert, St Jean du Gard
Link: Alais, Orange, Avignon
Recommended Excursions: [Walk] Langogne to Luc; [Car Tour] Florac to St Jean du Gard

3. The Mediterranean
Bases: Avignon or, say, Sisteron [three nights]
Visit: Avignon; [Nice], Menton; Hyères, [Marseilles]
Link: Montpellier, Millau, St Flour, Clermont Ferrand

4. Royat
Base: Royat [one/two nights]
Link: Vichy, Moulin, Nevers, Gien, Montargis, Nemours

5. Paris and Fontainebleau [four nights]
Visit: Barbizon, and Grès in the Forest of Fontainebleau [one or two days]
Visit: Luxembourg Gardens, Montparnasse, Musée Rodin, [Montmartre]

1. Fontainebleau

1.1 Barbizon

A. Musée Ganne	Old inn where an earlier generation of painters and writers used to congregate.
B. Maison de Rousseau	Municipal Museum, associated with the Musée d'Orsay in Paris with publications and exhibits connected with the painters of the Barbizon School.
C. Atelier Millet	Museum which includes references to, and photographs of, the painters who were in Barbizon at the same time as the Stevensons.
D. Hôtellerie de la Bas-Bréau	Called 'Stevenson's House' (plaque). An opulent hotel has replaced the older, simpler hotel, 'Siron's' or 'Hotel de l'Exposition' of Stevenson's day.
E. Rousseau-Millet Monument	Monument carved in a rock on the threshold of the Forest. It pays tribute to Barbizon's two most famous painters [buried at Chailly-en-Bière]. A nearby plaque connects them with contemporary concern for the environment and with the protection of the Forest.
F. Brigands' Cave	A short guided walk takes the visitor to a characteristic outcrop of weathered sandstone with massive blocks of rock and crevices, characteristic of the sort of scenery Stevenson describes in *Forest Notes*.

1.2 Grès

A. Hôtel Chevillon	Splendidly refurbished as a study centre by a Swedish Arts Foundation to celebrate the many Scandinavian artists who succeeded the Stevensons, and their friends.
B. Bridge	Celebrated subject of numerous pictures by many artists including Lavery. Stevenson and his friends picniced and played leap-frog on the lawns and swam and rowed in the river.
C. Delius's House	Lloyd Osbourne, RLS's step-son revisited Grèz, and met Delius in 1914.
D. Moret	RLS and Walter Simpson leaned on the Bridge at Moret while their barge, *The Eleven Thousand Virgins of Cologne*, was repaired.
E. Nemours	RLS and Belle Osbourne visited the riverside at Nemours.

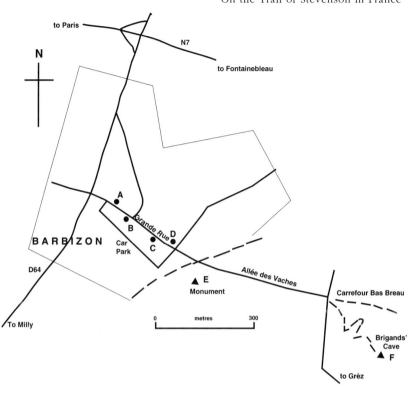

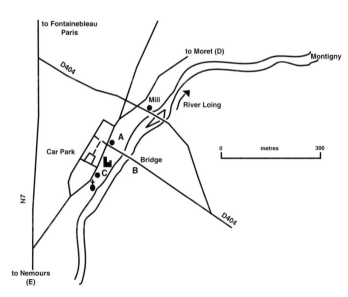

2. Inland Voyage

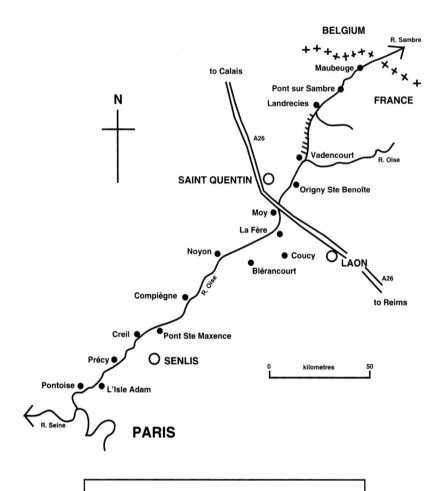

Locations shown on the map are described in the Gazetteer

3. Royat

A. Hôtel Continentale	Now an apartment block, affords views of the Spa Rooms and of the charming gardens in the centre of Royat. From the hotel RLS rode in a sedan chair down stairs leading to the springs.
B. Hôtel du Lyon	Centrally located hotel where RLS stayed on his second visit.
C. Spa	As elsewhere on the continent the spa is still very much alive, and the French Health Service devises suitable programmes of treatment for invalids. Nearby is the Tourist Office.
D. Musée du Passé	Pleasing small museum with much information about the history of Royat as a spa. Nearby is a splendid Romanesque church.

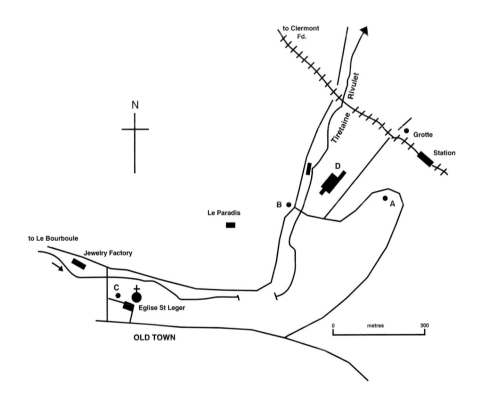

4. In the Cévennes

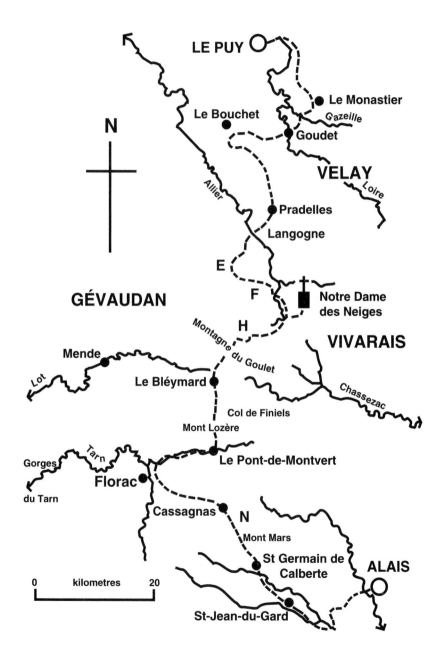

A. Le Monastier — Set above the Loire and dominated by a Benedictine abbey which houses a museum with a splendid Stevenson Room celebrating *Travels with a Donkey*. A Plinth opposite the Post Office marks the supposed starting point for RLS's now-famous journey. [Site of] Morel's Hotel is in the Place de la Fromagerie.

B. Goudet — Charming hamlet on the infant Loire. Beaufort Castle, where RLS first began to agonise about Modestine, commands a superb view.

C. Pradelles — A somewhat incongruous memorial to RLS exists in the 'Club Stevenson' a horse-riding establishment and night club.

D. Langogne — There are a few traces of the Old Bridge which RLS crossed, but the attractive old town centre is intact. Langogne is a good starting point for walkers.

E. Cheylard l'Evéque — Unspoiled hill village, probably much as it was in RLS's day.

F. Luc — RLS probably stayed at the inn near the station on the main road.

G. Notre Dame des Neiges — The modernised monastery is not very evocative, but will be deemed worth visiting because of the important part it played in *Travels*. Modestine's stable remains. Near La Bastide whence a walk, by forest paths, to Chasseradès is attractive.

H. Chasseradès — The viaduct which the navvies whom RLS met were building can still be seen.

J. Le Bléymard — Hamlet on the headwaters of the Lot. On his way from here to the summit of Mont Lozère RLS spent 'the night among the pines'.

K. Col de Finiels — Now a ski resort and walking centre, and thus somewhat lacking in C19 atmosphere.

L. Le Pont de Montvert — Hamlet on the upper Tarn, relatively unspoiled and welcoming. Good C18/19 bridge.

M. Cassagnas — Site of the 'Relais Stevenson', situated in an old railway station. The Mimette rivulet has several attractive rock pools.

N. Plan de Fontmort — Obelisk erected in 1887 to commemorate the centenary of the Edict of Tolerance.

Q. St-Jean-du-Gard — The small town on the Gardon where RLS left Modestine.

5. Menton

A. Hôtel Prince de Galles — Now situated in a parade of Grand Hotels rather than in splendid isolation it is difficult to imagine this hotel as RLS knew it, but it still has the Prince's Palace opposite it, and the tiny church which he so admired.

B. Bibliothèque — The record of visitors and celebrities makes some mention of Stevenson.

C. Bennet Monument, Rue Partouneaux — Monument to the English medical man who discovered the benefits of Menton.

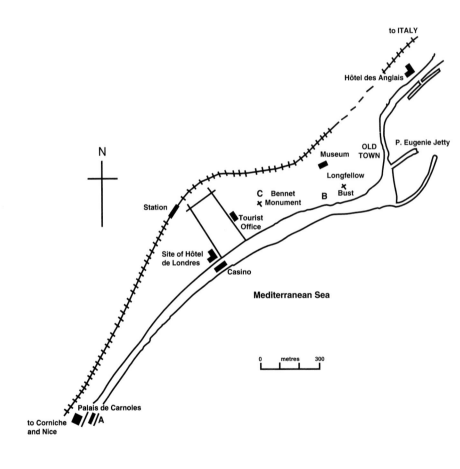

Bibliography

1. Books

BALFOUR, GRAHAM *The Life of Robert Louis Stevenson* 1901 [Methuen]

BILLCLIFFE, ROGER *The Glasgow Boys* 1985 [John Murray]

BROWN, GEORGE E *A Book of RLS* 1919 [Methuen]

CALDWELL, E.N. *Last Witness for...Stevenson* 1960 [Univ. of Oklahoma]

CAMPBELL, JULIAN *Frank O'Meara* 1989 [Hugh Lane AG Dublin]

CHARTERIS, EVAN *John Singer Sargent* 1931 [Heinemann]

CONNELL, JOHN *W.E. Henley* 1949 [Constable]

FIELD, ISOBEL *This Life I've Loved* 1937 [Michael Joseph]

FURNAS, J.C. *Voyage to Windward* 1952 [Faber & Faber]

HAMILTON, CLAYTON *On the Trail of Stevenson* 1916 [London]

HILL, ROBIN *RLS, Francophile* 1993 [Edinburgh]

JACOBS, MICHAEL *The Good and Simple Life* 1985 [Phaidon]

LAFORGE, M-T *Barbizon et l'Ecole de Barbizon* 1971 [Louvre, Paris]

LANG, ANDREW *Adventures Among Books* 1905 [Longmans]

LAVERY, SIR JOHN *The Life of a Painter* 1940 [London]

LOW, WILL H. *A Chronicle of Friendships* 1908 [Hodder & Stoughton]

MACKAY, MARGARET *The Violent Friend* 1969 [Dent]

MACKAY, AGNES *Arthur Melville – Scottish Impressionist* 1951 [Leigh-on-Sea]

MASSON, ROSALINE *I Can Remember Robert Louis Stevenson* 1925 [Chambers]

MILNER, JOHN *The Studios of Paris* 1988 [Yale]

MOUNT, CH. MERRILL	*John Singer Sargent* 1957 [The Cresset Press]
MOORE, GEORGE	*Confessions of a Young Man* 1888 [London]
OLSON, STANLEY	*John Singer Sargent – His Portrait* 1986 [MacMillan]
ORMOND, LEONÉE	*George Du Maurier* 1969 [Routledge Kegan Paul]
ORMOND, RICHARD	*John Singer Sargent* 1970 [Phaidon]
RANKIN, ANDREW	*Dead Man's Chest* 1987 [Faber]
SANCHEZ, N.V. DE G.	*Mrs Robert Louis Stevenson* 1920 [Chatto & Windus]
SAROLEA, CHARLES	*Robert Louis Stevenson and France* 1923
SIMPSON, E.B.	*The R.L. Stevenson Originals* 1912 [Foulis]
SMITH, JANET A.	*R.L. Stevenson – Collected Poems* 1971 [Rupert Hart Davis]
STEVENSON, R.A.M.	*Velasquez* [Edited by Denys Sutton]
STEVENSON, R.L.	*Collected Works* 1923 [Tusitala Edition]
	Letters [Volumes I-II]; New Arabian Nights; The Merry Men and Other Tales; Further Memories; Across the Plains; An Inland Voyage; etc.
STEVENSON, R.L. AND OSBOURNE, L.	*The Wrecker* 1892 [London]
SWEARINGEN, ROGER	*The Prose Writings of...Stevenson* 1980 [Connecticut]
TREGLOWN, J.	*The Lantern Bearers and Other Essays* 1988 [Chatto & Windus]

2. Articles and Pamphlets

DAPLYN, A.J.	*RLS at Barbizon* [Chambers Journal, July 1917]
GAZEAU-CAILLE, M-T.	*Landscape Painters at Barbizon* [Barbizon, 1989]
HARRISON, BIRGE	*With Stevenson at Grèz* [Century Magazine 1917]
MCCONKEY, KENNETH	*From Grèz to Glasgow* [Sc. Arts Rev. XV No 4 1982]
MEHEW, E.J.	Two Uncollected Stevenson Contributions to the Magazine 'London' [*The Stevensonian* Aug 1965]
PENNELL, JOSEPH	*RLS Illustrator* [Studio 1896/7]
SADLER, F.	*L'Hôtel Chevillon et les Artistes de Grèz sur Loing* [Grèz 1938]
STEVENSON, R.A.M.	*William Stott* [Magazine of Art 1900]
STEVENSON, R.A.M.	*Grèz* [Magazine of Art 1893]

Acknowledgements

Work of this sort preys on the work of others. I readily acknowledge the work of all of those authors mentioned in the bibliography who have considered the way in which Stevenson lived in France. I am particularly grateful to friends in Britain, and in France, who have helped me.

Index

F

Ferrier, Coggie, 94
Ferrier, James W, 28, 94
Flaubert, Gustav (1821-80), 14
France, Anatole (Jacques Thibault), 14
Furnas, J. C., 47, 49

G

Gaboriau, Emile (1832-73), 15

H

Hamerton, Philip Gilbert, 6
Harrison, Alexander (1853-1930), 64, 75
Harrison, Lowell Birge (1854-1929), 17, 18, 20, 21, 65, 68
Hawkins, Louis Weldon (d. 18002-85), 17, 23, 65
Henley, Wm. E., 18, 46, 53, 54, 61, 94, 103
Hugo, Victor-Marie (1802-85), 12, 13, 34

I

Inland Voyage, An, 7, 8, 50, 56, 64, 72, 74, 97

J

James, Henry, 11
Jameson, Middleton (d.1919), 21, 61

L

Lang, Andrew, 8, 11, 12, 15, 34, 35, 36
Lavery, John, 21, 22, 23, 58
Low, Will H., 38, 39, 41, 48, 53, 58, 61, 69, 70,
    71, 73, 75, 79, 80, 91, 95, 101
Løwstädt, Emma, 65

M

Michelet, Jules (1798-1874), 14, 93
Millet, 58, 59
Molière, Jean Baptiste Poquelin (1622-73), 14
Montaigne, Michel E. de (1533-92), 12, 14
Montépin, Xavier de (1823-1902), 15
Munkacsy, Mihaly (1844-1900), 61
Murger, Henri (1822-61), 14, 39, 60
Musset, Alfred de (1810-57), 14

O

O'Meara, Frank, 20, 23, 42, 46, 59
Orléans, Charles d' (1391-1465), 13
Osbourne, Lloyd, 5, 8, 24, 45, 70, 71, 79, 98

Chateau Beaufort from Goudet sun Loire.

***Chateau Beaufort: drawing by RLS of what turned out to be the first stop on
his** Travels with a Donkey*